Hardrock Fever:

Running 100 Miles in Colorado's San Juan Mountains

To William —
Keep the faith !
Never give up !

Bob Boeder

Hardrock Fever:

Running 100 Miles in Colorado's San Juan Mountains

Robert B. Boeder

Old Mountain Press

Published by:
Old Mountain Press, Inc.
2542 S. Edgewater Dr.
Fayetteville, NC 28303

www.oldmp.com

© 2000 Robert B. Boeder
Front cover photo by Eric Robinson,
Back cover photo by Judy Esser
ISBN: 1-884778-84-4
Library of Congress Catalog Card Number: 00-190206

Hardrock Fever.

First Edition
Manufactured in the United States of America
1 2 3 4 5 6 7 8 9 10

CONTENTS

Book 1

The San Juans

Write the vision;
Make it plain on tablets,
So he may run who reads it.

Habakkuk 1:2.2

I'm sitting on the ground in Hillside Cemetery in Silverton, Colorado. The graveyard lies on the south- facing, lower slope of Storm Mountain and is perched above a RV park and the Animas River. On the other side of the river (originally called *La Piedra de los Animas*–The River of Lost Souls) I can see the abandoned Lackawanna Mine mill at the foot of Swansea Gulch. The mill isn't far from Arrastra Gulch, where the first gold and silver discoveries in the San Juan Mountains were made in the 1870's. Silverton is situated in a valley at the confluence of the Animas River with Cement Creek and Mineral Creek. Besides Storm Mountain, the other sentinels guarding the flanks of the small town are Kendall Mountain rising in front of me, Sultan Mountain to the southwest, and Anvil Mountain to the northwest. Each of these peaks reaches over 13,000 feet while Silverton is 9,318 feet above sea level.

The cemetery contains over 3,000 graves, but it teems with life. The townspeople maintain the burial grounds of their forefathers only sporadically, so weeds and flowers, especially daisies, grow abundantly, sharing the place with alder and pine trees and the sound of rushing water. A chipmunk scurries by on a food search. A green and red broad-tailed hummingbird hovers near me, its wings a blur. Birds call, cicadas drone, flies buzz around me, and ants are crawling up my legs. Getting up to brush them off, I wander around examining the graves.

A small statue of the Virgin Mary protects the final resting place of Joseph Robert Davenport, who lived for just two days, from July 8 to July 10, 1977. Joseph lies next to Junebelle Anna Adlee, SSGT, US Army, WW II, June 4, 1915, to September 14, 1995. Many of the grave sites are enclosed by iron fences. As if feeding on the remains buried beneath them, large trees are growing right out of some of the plots. High on the hillside is a stone for Annie Mary Miles, who died on October 29, 1889, at the age of 9 months and 18 days. George Parker Plantz, Pioneer of San Juan County, 1850 to 1936, is buried here. So is Frank Babich, who died in the flu epidemic of 1918 that killed 10 percent of Silverton's population in less than a month. The burial place of Herman Dalla (April 15, 1912 – May 23, 1997) is adorned with a Colorado Rockies batting helmet.

It's July 5, 1999, and I've journeyed to Silverton on my annual pilgrimage to participate in the Hardrock 100 Mile Endurance Run. This will be my fourth attempt to complete this wildest and toughest of all the 100 mile trail races. After three failures, I have become obsessed with Hardrock. Some necessity of my heart brings me back to the San Juans each summer. I can't say that I understand it. Perhaps it's the raw power of the San Juan landscape. All I know is that being here makes me happy.

In many ways the Hardrock Hundred is about chasing the ghosts of time past. Hanging out in the cemetery is my way of paying homage to the people the race celebrates—the

Hardrock miners. It gives me a certain perspective on the town, its history and geography, and it is also a place where I can be alone with my thoughts about Joel Zucker, who died after finishing the 1998 race.

John DeWalt and I were the last runners to see Joel alive when he left Silverton at 10 a.m. on the Monday after the race with his pacer, Brian Scott, and Brian's family. They were driving to the Albuquerque airport to catch Joel's flight back home to New York state. Joel was tired following another stirring Hardrock finish, but we talked together and joked and he seemed normal. Four hours later—at the age of 44 and in great physical condition—he was dead of a brain hemorrhage. I was a friend of Joel's, but not one of his ace buddies. We saw each other twice a year, in April at the Umstead 100 mile race (held in Umstead State Park near Cary, North Carolina, not far from my home in Fayetteville) then here in Silverton for Hardrock in July. He didn't shower me with e-mail messages like he did those people he really liked. But Joel had a charisma about him. An unusually close bond links the runners who tackle the Hardrock, and I respected him as a three-time finisher of the race.

Joel reminded me of a Tommyknocker. Tommyknockers are like elves and leprechauns. Their stories were brought to America from England by Cornish miners in the nineteenth century, then embellished with other traditions as the miners moved west to Colorado and the San Juans. Tommyknockers can be evil, but mostly they are friendly and sometimes mischievous. The spirits of men who have died in mine accidents become Tommyknockers. They want to be remembered fondly and be left some food and drink. If satisfied, they save men's lives during disasters and lead them to discover wealthy veins of precious minerals. Sometimes they can be heard and seen working in remote parts of mines in utter darkness, damp and cold. Tommyknockers have big heads and big feet, beards, long arms and short legs and bodies–kind of like Joel except for the beard. Maybe Joel was some sort of renegade fresh-air Tommyknocker who had left the mine and taken up trail running. He had a lot of Tommyknocker characteristics, and runners share the same kind of camaraderie as did miners.

The last thing Joel said to me before he left Silverton with Brian Scott was, "Bob, some people just aren't meant to finish Hardrock." Joel could be painfully frank. After he died, I often wondered if he had put some kind of Tommyknocker whammy on me and I was doomed to a lifetime of Hardrock DNFs (Did Not Finish in running parlance).

The Hardrock 100 mile endurance run, the highest and most scenic of all the 100 mile trail ultras, takes runners through the San Juan Mountains with their peaks and crags, alpine meadows, bounding streams and unpredictable weather. The course circles from the old mining community of Silverton to the ski resort town of Telluride to spectacular Ouray then back to Silverton. Thirteen summits in the San Juans exceed 14,000 feet, and hundreds of peaks rise above 12,000 feet. Timberline occurs between 11,000 and 11,500 feet. Much of the Hardrock course is above timberline in lofty terrain that is barren, rocky, and inhospitable.

Surrounded by semi-arid regions of Colorado, Utah, and New Mexico, the San Juans are a place of heavy summer thunderstorms and deep winter snows. The moisture is carried across hundreds of miles of desert on prevailing southwesterly winds that strike the mountains head on, dumping over 200 inches of snow a year on the high country passes.

The Animas River is the main drainage channel for the high central San Juans around Silverton. The Animas surges south into New Mexico, where it joins the westward flowing San Juan River that eventually mixes with the waters of the Colorado River in Lake Powell. The Uncompahgre River drains the northern section of the San Juans and joins the Gunnison River which wanders northward before entering the Colorado River at Grand Junction.

The Continental Divide bisects the San Juans. The race takes place mostly on the western side of the divide, but

9

runners cross and recross it between the 70 and 85 mile points just above Cataract Lake and again before descending to Maggie Gulch.

The San Juans are sub-divided into four ranges: the Needles and the Grenadier Ranges fifteen miles south of Silverton, the Sneffels Range west of Ouray, and the Silverton Range north of town. Each has its own geologic significance and unique topography. The Needles Range is made of granite, the Grenadiers of contorted and upturned quartzite layers, the two others carved by ancient glaciers out of volcanic rock. Curiosity about geology and high altitude trail running go together.

The San Juans constitute one of the greatest natural geological laboratories in the world. The oldest San Juan rocks were formed 1.8 billion years ago, time beyond human comprehension. In some places near Ouray, 500 million years of geologic history-from Cambrian time to the present-are laid bare in a continuous sequence on the canyon walls. Layering on the walls represents the shorelines of ancient seas which repeatedly inundated the Western Hemisphere from Mexico to Alaska, depositing layers of sand, soil, and fossils before receding gradually only to repeat the process.

Geologic forces arched the original flat-lying rocks of the region upward 65 million years ago into a dome-like giant blister on the earth's crust that was exposed to severe erosion, which removed the upper layers to expose the core of the dome. This is the basement, the older cystalline rocks usually buried under sedimentary cover.

Eighteen huge volcanoes formed in the eastern San Juans 30 million years ago and began violently spewing red hot, gas-laden ash. Repeatedly, the volcanoes filled with ash and debris then emptied, building up their cones then collapsing. In these collapsed volcanoes, called calderas, mineralized fluids seeped into fractures and fissures depositing veins of gold, silver, cooper, lead, and zinc. The Silverton caldera-just north of town, bounded by the Animas River and Mineral Creek, and loaded with rich veins of mineral wealth-is the ancient throat of one of these volcanoes. The Hardrock 100 course basically takes runners in a wide circle around the Silverton caldera.

Beginning a couple of million years ago, ice piled up in the polar regions, the earth's climate became cooler and wetter, and snow fell building up permanent snow fields. Annual layers of snow compressed and became glaciers that gradually swept down hills under the burden of their own weight. These glaciers scraped out U-shaped valleys. Glaciers also created bowl-shaped hollows, called cirques, on mountainsides. When the glaciers melted they left small lakes, called tarns, at the bottom of each cirque. When cirques formed on three or more sides of a mountain, the remnant peak was often shaped like a horn—the Matterhorn in the Swiss Alps being the most famous example. In the San Juans, Mt. Sneffels and Golden Horn in the Silverton Range are this type of peak.

As the glaciers melted, they dumped piles of boulders, sand, and mud (called moraines) at the end of the glacier and along the sides where they formed ridges. The last glaciers melted 15,000 years ago leaving rivers to erode valleys so sometimes U-shaped upper valleys have V-shaped canyons cut in their floors.

While the mountains were being formed, primitive horses, camels, and tigers roamed nearby. Gradually these animals were replaced by bear, elk, deer, goats, and mountain sheep. The abundance of animals drew Ute and Paiute Native Americans into the region, followed later by Navajo. The Ute began as nomadic hunter-gatherers; then they adopted agriculture and started weaving and making pots. The introduction of the horse into the southwest by the Spanish in the late 1500's completely altered the Ute lifestyle. They ceased all of their previous economic activities. The horse gave them mobility; they were able to hunt and kill large numbers of bison on the plains and transport their belongings over long distances. Established Ute migratory routes became wilderness highways, followed later by explorers and prospectors. With the horse the Ute became warriors renowned for their bravery.

Traditional Ute territory included all of Colorado and most of Utah plus parts of Kansas, Nebraska, Oklahoma, Wyoming, New Mexico, and Arizona. Their favorite wintering place was at the Garden of the Gods near Colorado Springs, and Manitou Springs was their sacred ground. At the core of Ute religion was the concept of obtaining power and guidance from the sun, moon, stars, plants, and animals. A symbol of the person's power source decorated his tepee and clothing. Eagles were especially important animals. Wearing eagle feathers in war bonnets conferred bravery on Ute warriors. Living in harmony with their fellow Ute, with nature and with the creator was the goal of life on earth.

The harmonious theme did not extend to their neighbors. The Ute believed that the Great Spirit approved of hunting and war, so they fought with the Navajo and Comanche, raided the Paiute, and sold slaves to the Spanish. Ute culture peaked in the 1840's then underwent major changes in the next fifty years as the Indians collided with growing numbers of white men invading the mountains. Indians and whites had different concepts of how to relate to their surroundings. The Indians trod lightly on the earth. The mountains had spiritual significance for them whereas the whites viewed the land materialistically. For Indians, land ownership meant simply the right to roam the mountains, to enjoy them as they did the sunlight and the wind in their faces. They had no clue about the legal aspects of acquiring real estate and mineral rights. Whites wanted to make maximum use of the land. This meant farming, mining, and individual property rights. Communal ownership, wandering around, fishing, hunting and gathering- the basis of the Indian economy-didn't count. The inevitable collision between the white and the Indian way of life came in the 1870's. Ute country was loaded with gold and silver, and when push came to shove, the Indians were outgunned and lost out. By 1880 the Ute had been confined to two reservations in northeastern Utah and one in southwestern Colorado. Hard rock miners had taken over the San Juans.

The "Run Principles" section of the Hardrock 100 sign-up sheet informs applicants, "The run is a salute to the toughness and perseverance of the hard rock miners who initially developed the area." I have no problem admiring the toughness of anyone that has ever lived and worked in the San Juans, but I'm not sure if "developed" is the right word for what the mining industry did to the mountains. It was more like indecent assault. In 1871, George Howard led an exploratory group of prospectors into the Animas River region. Lacking the supplies to spend a winter in the San Juans, they returned in 1872 to establish the Little Giant mine in Arrastra Gulch.

Placer mining, the comparatively simple way of recovering gold from streams and rivers that rewarded miners handsomely in California, did not work in Arrastra Gulch. The mining method that was required in the San Juans was lode or vein mining. The term "lode" refers to an open fissure in the earth caused by an ancient earthquake or volcanic action that later filled with mineral-bearing fluids. The rock of the San Juans is extremely hard manganese and quartz. Miners would hike up the gulches looking for white quartz outcroppings tinted by the rusty color that signifies the presence of gold. Once they located such an outcropping, they would stake their claims and begin work. In order to free the precious metals from the earth, miners needed to use drills and explosives to break and crush the rock that was then washed for gold.

Initially, drilling was done by hand using a four pound hammer and a chisel, called a drill steel. Miners swung the hammer with one hand, hitting the steel then twisting it an eighth of an inch and repeating the process. This was called single jacking. A good man could drill 12 inches in 30 minutes, and this went on for 10 hours per shift. With double jacking, two men worked together, one swinging a 6-8 pound hammer, the other holding and rotating the steel to keep the hole round. Partners switched jobs every 7-10 minutes and averaged 40-60 hits per minute. This method produced a 30-inch hole in a half-hour. A number of holes were drilled in a pattern, filled with powder, and fired. Firing was an art because the holes had to ignite in a particular sequence so that they all exploded completely and all the rock was broken. The broken rock, called muck, was removed and the whole process repeated. Two men working ten hours a day could advance a tunnel five feet wide and seven feet high six feet a day. The pay was $3 per day, $2 if you lived at the mine. Sometimes men were killed when dynamite exploded at the wrong time or they were hit by falling rock.

Air compressors changed mining. The first air-driven drills were dry drills with no water to retard the dust that went right into the miners' lungs, killing them eventually. Wet drills were introduced to eliminate the dust and to cool the bit as it was drilling while also washing the cuttings from the powder hole.

Silverton, Howardsville, Eureka, and other towns quickly sprouted in the mountain valleys. They served as supply and transport centers for mines high in the mountains. Initially, all supplies were carried on the backs of mules, burros, and horses. The broken rock containing the highest percentage of gold was loaded onto the animals for the return trip to the towns and river valleys where mills were built to process the ore. Trams were constructed at the larger mines. Over fifty trams were built in San Juan County. One of the most spectacular and the only one with steel towers was the 10,100 foot long Shenandoah tram, which carried fifty-two buckets and dropped from 11,200 feet at the mine in Arrastra Gulch to 9,700 feet at the mill site on the Animas River. Sometimes avalanches tore down the tram towers. To divert the snow, slide splitters were constructed just uphill from the towers. Miners rode the trams to work in all kinds of weather throughout the year.

Single men lived in boarding houses at the mine and went to town once a month. Married miners rode the tram down to the road after their shifts and made their way to their homes in town. Some of the mine buildings–bunkhouses, tram houses, machine shops–were perched precariously on cliffs and steep mountainsides. Buildings were constructed on platforms connected with wooden walkways. The buildings were tied to the rock walls with steel cables bolted to pieces of steel that were cemented in holes drilled in the rock so they wouldn't be swept away by avalanches, rockslides, or wild weather.

Many of the first miners were immigrants from Scotland, Ireland, and England, especially Cornwall. They were followed by Swedes and Finns. Then came the Austrians from Tyrol and Italians from the provinces of Piedmont and Tuscany. They worked for weeks or months in the mines until the need for human interaction drew them to Silverton, which had become the main gathering place for miners. An imaginary line down the center of Greene Street separated the "liquor side" (east of the line) from the "society" section to the west, where the good church-going folk lived. The east side of Greene was lined with saloons like The Crystal Palace, The Rose Bud, and The Arlington, where Wyatt Earp managed the gambling rooms for a year in 1883. Blair Street was the red light district, where working girls were available and bars were open 24 hours a day, year round. The bars offered drinking, gambling, dancing and fighting–all the excitement missing from life in the mountains. By 1882 Silverton hosted 29 saloons and at least 117 prostitutes. The girls had descriptive names like Broken Nose Grace, Irish Nell, Minnie the Baby Jumbo, and Diamond Tooth Leona.

Outside of marriage or ill paying menial jobs like dress maker or house servant, there weren't many occupational choices for women in a mining town 100 years ago, so many single girls with no means of support turned to prostitution. They weren't supposed to solicit openly on the streets, so the girls worked either in groups out of bordellos or independently in small one or two room buildings, called cribs. If their doors were ajar and the red lights were on, they were open for business.

The girls underwent weekly medical examinations that kept sexually transmitted diseases under control. Alcoholism, depression, and suicide were common among both miners and prostitutes. Many of the women became addicted to morphine and opium. Occasionally, black faces peer out of early photographs of life in Silverton. "Nigger" Lola became the favorite date of many Silverton businessmen. For years Chinese immigrants operated laundries and restaurants in Silverton. In the local newspapers Orientals were always referred to in derogatory terms as "pigtailed heathens." Hard working people, their one failing was their devotion to opium smoking. At the turn of the century, miners' unions became strongly anti-Chinese because they were afraid the mine owners would import cheap Chinese labor, so in 1902 Silverton unions called for a boycott of Chinese businesses. The same thing happened in other Colorado mining towns like Leadville, Cripple Creek, and Colorado Springs. Those Chinese who didn't flee were thrown out of town.

Silverton wasn't a town with an outlaw reputation like Dodge City or Tombstone. It was the epitome of a place where somebody could make a living through hard work and sweat. Town ordinances established penalties for gambling and prostitution. Every month the bar owners and the girls traipsed over to city hall to pay their fines. This was the cost of doing business in town, and the proceeds financed local government.

The hopes of early miners for major gold strikes were not realized but the mountains were full of silver, lead, copper, and zinc. In order to make a profit on these minerals, miners had to mill large tonnages of ore, more than could be brought down on the backs of pack animals. With the arrival of the Denver and Rio Grande narrow gauge railway in Silverton in 1882, mining in the San Juans really boomed. Transportation became cheaper and faster, lower grade ore could be shipped, and heavy machinery could be brought in. More mines, mills, and smelters opened up as branch lines were constructed up the Animas River valley, into Cunningham Gulch, up Cement Creek to Gladstone, and up Mineral Creek to Red Mountain. All this economic activity came to a screeching halt in 1893 when the government demonetized silver and the market crashed. A couple of years later, the mining industry was back on its feet with better milling practices for base metal recovery and the discovery of gold-bearing veins that brought big time capitalists like the Rockefellers and Guggenheims into the mining industry. The best years for Silverton were the first decade of the twentieth century. The population of San Juan County reached 5000, taxes were rolling in, and most of the town and county public buildings were erected at that time.

Prohibition in the 1920's couldn't close the Silverton bars, but the depression of the 1930's shut down the mining industry and everything else in town. Except for the line from Durango, the railroads pulled up their tracks. In 1948, Jew Fanny, the last prostitute in Silverton, left town because, as she put it, "You can't sell it when they're giving it away for free." In the 1950's a couple of western movies, one called Ticket to Tomahawk, were made in Silverton, but nothing else was happening. The re-opening of the Sunnyside mine in 1959 saved the town from extinction. In 1991, the Sunnyside closed permanently, the tunnels were sealed with concrete plugs, and the mining era ended. During the decade of the 1990's San Juan County lost 25 percent of its population, the highest decline of any county in the continental U.S.

Few people made millions from mining. The common working men lived from paycheck to paycheck. Many mining companies failed financially because they made the mistake of spending a lot of money on mills, trams, and equipment before enough mineral bearing ore was found to justify the costs. Town merchants and bar owners who controlled the women achieved the greatest financial success. And the yields from hard rock mining were miniscule compared with what an open pit mine could produce.

Hindsight is always 20/20 and it may be unfair to judge one era by the standards of another, but from the environmental standpoint, the miners left a real mess in the San Juans. Ruined mine buildings and abandoned equipment litter the countryside. Some of the buildings, like the Old Hundred boarding house perched high on the slopes of Galena Mountain, are wonderful to behold, but others like the concrete footings of the old mill marching up the hillside in Eureka are eyesores. Mine dumps, the rock dug from mines that was never processed, disfigure every mountainside. Minerals leaching from the dumps constitute a threat to the water supply. Open mine tunnels invite pets and hikers into dangerous situations where explosive or poisonous gases and oxygen-deficient atmospheres can kill people.

Now the high country peaks and basins are quiet. No more shouts of miners and clangs of trams fill the air. The only sounds are the howling of the wind and the polyphony of rushing water. In the year 2000, Silverton boasts 350 year-round residents which increases to around 700 in the summer when the Durango and Silverton Narrow Gauge Railroad brings over 200,000 tourists to town from May to October. When the trains stop running, most businesses board up their windows and winter sets in—long, cold, and snowbound. But eventually summer returns bringing cyclists and runners to the San Juans for the Iron Horse 47 mile bicycle race from Durango to Silverton in late May, the Kendall Mountain 13 Mile Run in late July, and the Hardrock 100 Mile Endurance Run in mid-July. That's why I'm here.

Book 2

Preparation

"People who like this sort of thing will find this the sort of thing they like."
                    Sir Max Beerbohm.

T he first time the Hardrock 100 ever caught my attention was when I read an article in the September 1992 issue of *Ultrarunning* magazine written by Jim Fisher about the initial running of the race. Several sentences in that article stood out. Among them were:

"This event includes stretches where runners make life and death decisions with each step....I freaked out so badly during this run that I was virtually babbling incoherently for two days to anyone who would listen....I have never been that terrified in my 41 years.... This is a survival run. This doesn't mean surviving to the finish line. This means surviving period."

The race sounded like fun. I didn't know Fisher, but he was an experienced mountain trail ultrarunner who DNFed the 1992 Hardrock at 67 miles after 29 hours suffering from prune feet.

The three other articles about Hardrock '92 in that issue of *Ultrarunning* written by David Horton, Ulli Kamm, and

Gordon Hardman, the race director were slightly less hysterical. In fact, Ulli sounded like he had fallen in love when he wrote:

"It is now three days since I finished this fantastic race, but I still can't stop thinking about it....It is exactly what I have been looking for since I started ultras (129 finished so far)....It is the trail race of a lifetime."

Horton's article pointed out some problems the race had with course markings. It seems that marmots, large woodchuck-like rodents with short legs and bushy tails that live above tree line, love the taste of plastic and devoured course markers as quickly as they were put down. Not to be outdone, elk mistook the marking flags for flowers, picked them up, then spat them out on the ground when they turned out to be too chewy. In addition, the weather was terrible, with cold rain and wind during both nights and the second day. East coast runners David Horton and Nancy Hamilton won the 1992 race with Dennis Herr taking second overall. The legendary Rick Trujillo of Ouray, Colorado, who pioneered the Imogene Pass race and won the Pike's Peak Marathon five straight years from 1973-77, was forced to drop out due to overextended quads. Of the 42 who started only 18 finished.

Normally, I bypass first time races because they usually have kinks to work out. I also avoid races with reputations for poorly marked courses, so I didn't mind missing Hardrock for the first few years until the race managers solved some of their logistics difficulties. When they dreamed up this event, the Hardrock organizers decided to change course directions every year, mimicking the Comrades Marathon in South Africa. In 1992, the race was run clockwise. The general consensus of runners that have completed the race in both directions multiple times is that clockwise is less difficult than counterclockwise. The reasons are that there are more long downhill sections going clockwise and that three of the toughest climbs in the race–Oscar's Pass, Virginius Pass, and Grant-Swamp Pass-come in the second half of the counterclockwise course. Either way, the cumulative vertical gain of over 33,000 feet doesn't change and the average elevation of over 11,000 feet remains the same. Charlie Thorn, one of the primary course architects since the race's inception, claims that both directions are equally easy.

In 1993, Jim Fisher returned to Silverton and finished the counterclockwise run in 43:21. His *Ultrarunning* article about the '93 Hardrock adopted a different tone from his '92 effort:

"This run is still very difficult, very hazardous, and should not be taken lightly. But if you get above all the hard, dirty, grubby work and terror of falling off cliffs, you will find incredible beauty."

Fisher's '92 article may have scared some runners away from Hardrock '93 because only 34 started, but 26 finished, perhaps the highest finishing percentage of any 100 mile trail race. David Horton won the '93 race in the still standing record time of 29:35. Horton was followed by Charlie Thorn in 32:36. Margaret Smith of Missoula, Montana, took the women's title. Late in the race Nancy Hamilton neglected to take enough warm clothes with her for the big climb to the top of Grant-Swamp Pass and wound up with a severe case of hypothermia. She required help to return safely to Chapman aid station. Ulli Kamm and his wife, Traudl, journied from Germany to the San Juans again. He finished in 44:38. In 1993, Dennis Herr took nine hours out of the race to sleep in Ouray then made a spectacular "return from the dead" gallop over the final 40 miles to finish in sixth place in 35:52. If that nine hours in the sleeping bag are subtracted from his finishing time, he holds the unofficial course record.

The course marking problems of 1992 were solved the next year by 3000 special marmot-proof 3" by 3" squares of tin covered with yellow reflective tape attached to three foot long pieces of stiff wire. Instructions in blue lettering were printed on the tape. On one side was written, "Hardrock 100 Trail Marker. PLEASE DO NOT REMOVE before July 30." On the other side was the run logo plus "Conducted under

USFS and BLM permits. Questions: Call Silverton Chamber of Commerce 387-5654."

Dennis Herr's new look after falling on his face in the San Juans. Photo by Bob Boeder

Fluttering in the breeze, the markers worked well enough although they could be mistaken for alpine flowers. At night they stood out when caught in flashlight beams from a distance. Difficulties remained with the elk who don't read well and continued to take pleasure in trampling the markers into the mountain meadow muck and mire.

In 1994, David Horton recorded a rare DNF opening the way for first time 100 miler, Scott Hirst, to win the race in 32 hours. Hirst was closely followed by Rick Trujillo who finally got in good enough shape to make it all the way around and finished in 32:40. Margaret Smith repeated as the women's champ in 38:43. Word that the course markings had improved had spread in the ultrarunning community and 75 runners showed up although only 37 finished.

Each year at Hardrock, a local artist paints a scene from the course; the painting is printed and the reprints are awarded to each finisher. Until 1999 the scene was screened onto the backs of the official race shirts. Silver gold-mining pans are given to the winners, and the Caboose award goes to the final finisher. In addition, the annual Mother Lode award recognizes an individual who contributes greatly to the success of the run.

Too much snow cancelled the race in 1995. The town of Silverton averages around 180 inches of snow each year–that's 15 feet. The high passes receive much more. Traditionally, snowpacks in the San Juans are prone to avalanches. Paths taken by the snow slides are clearly visible on the mountainsides. Many of them have their own names. Weak snowpacks are caused by early snow followed by a long pause in precipitation and low overnight temperatures. Large, poorly bonded snow crystals lie at the bottom of the snowpack. These crystals act like ball bearings. When they are disturbed, the snow on top of them rolls down the mountain slopes sweeping away everything in its path.

Beginning in early June, the snowpack begins melting and the snow vanishes rapidly. Most years on race day there will be snow on the north slopes of the high basins and passes. The amount depends on how much snow falls in late spring during the months of March, April, and May. In 1995, a total of 100 inches fell during those three months for a total accumulation of 243 inches. The high country was inaccessible and the race had to be cancelled. In 1993, the year's total was 273 inches, but most of that fell before March. As a result, there was little snow on the course and the race was held.

In the spring of 1996 I started thinking about entering Hardrock. In 1994 I had done the Grand Slam of trail ultrarunning, finishing four 100 mile races in the space of 14 weeks so I felt confident. I held off applying until early June; then, inexplicably, I had this overpowering urge to sign up for the race. I telephoned race organizer Christine Bass, and she said they were full but I could send in my money and get on the waiting list. I didn't fully realize it at the time, but I had caught the Hardrock fever just like Ulli Kamm, Kirk Apt, Bert Meyer, and the other runners who keep turning up in Silverton every year in early July.

Christine mailed me the Hardrock Hundred Runners Manual. While reading through it, I paused at the section devoted to weather:

The weather is a dominant factor for this run and is at least as formidable as the terrain, remoteness, or high altitude. It is our general opinion that the first fatality we have will be either from hypothermia or lightning!....The run date is a compromise between other mountain trail runs on the calendar and the weather. There is a period of a few days to weeks each year when the snow is generally gone, but the summer 'monsoon' has not yet gotten into full swing–we try to hit this window. Prepare for any amount of snow! We could even have more snow just before the run....Remember, there have been avalanche fatalities in Colorado in every month of the year except September.

Repetition of the word *fatality* made me wonder, but I kept reading until I paused again at the 11-page, single-spaced course description. Eleven pages! More detail even than the Wasatch Front 100 miler course description. What impressed me more was the frequent repetition of the words "*Acrophobia* and *Exposure*" in the text. There must be at least half a dozen places on the course where anyone with an abnormal fear of heights will be in a good position to fall a long way with a wrong step.

I'm not sure where "healthy respect" stops and "abnormal fear" begins. When I was a little kid I was scared of heights. Whenever I was in my parent's car and they drove over a high bridge, I covered my head with my arms and cowered on the floor of the back seat. I've progressed to the point now where I get a cheap thrill from driving over those same bridges, but I'm not someone who enjoys sitting on the edge of Grand Canyon dangling his legs over the abyss.

That first attempt in '96 turned out to be a real fiasco. Since I had finished the Leadville 100 miler twice with no altitude-related problems, I thought I could get by with a week's acclimatization. And that's all the time I could spare since I was the director of a 10K race on July 4 in Fayetteville, and Hardrock was on the weekend of July 10-12. So after the 10K I flew out to Denver along with my son, Steve, who agreed to crew for me. We rented a car, spent a couple of days in Leadville, then drove down to Silverton.

Once in town we checked into the Triangle Motel on Greene Street and moved into a two bedroom suite with a kitchen and living room. Suzi Thibeault (now Suzi Cope) was preparing for her fourth attempt to finish the race, and the day after arriving I joined her group for a training run. I enjoyed the fellowship with the other runners, all Hardrock veterans, but, being trail dumb, I had no clue what they were talking about when they referred to the various passes, gulches, and aid stations on the course. This problem continued at the long briefing on Wednesday before the race. I had read the course description in the runners' manual, but there were just too many new place names for me to remember and they all seemed to have their own eccentricities. And I was still concerned about course markings.

Thursday at runner check-in at the EMT office was the first time I ever saw Joel Zucker. He was in a characteristic pose down on his hands and knees exchanging a deep soul kiss with somebody's dog. I thought this was terrific so I yelled across the room,

"You know dogs lick their genitals at least eight times every day, don't you?"

Joel looked up and shouted back, "Ya, but her breath is sweeter than yours."

By race day I was a bundle of nerves and decided whenever possible to hook up with someone who knew the course and stay with them no matter what so I wouldn't get lost. The race that year was run counterclockwise, so the first aid station was Cunningham Gulch, where I made two big mistakes. The first was drinking two 8-ounce cans of Ensure Plus one after the other. The second was deciding to wear a backpack for the first time ever in a race. Since there was lots of room in the backpack I filled it with everything I thought I would need for the race. The backpack was way too heavy.

Steve is the best crewman I've had in all my races, always enthusiastic and thinking ahead. Staggering out of the aid station under the weight of my pack I could only respond with a weak wave when he yelled, "Go Dad." Crew access at Hardrock is limited to six of the twelve aid stations. When I reached the second aid station at Maggie's Gulch, which is closed to crews, I was in trouble. Jogging downhill I slipped on the wet grass and took a nasty fall that knocked a lot of the eagerness for mountain running out of me. And I felt lousy, bloated and nauseous, because the two Ensures I had consumed at Cunningham were just sitting in my stomach doing nothing. Evidently, I didn't have the necessary sodium in my system to digest them. So when I arrived at the aid station, I was unresponsive when Andi Kron spoke to me. An experienced aid station worker knows something is wrong when a runner isn't talking. Andi thought I was suffering from altitude sickness and wanted to pull me from the race, but I assured her that wasn't my problem. After lying down for 20 minutes, I threw up the Ensures. Vomiting made me feel a lot better and I continued.

On the next section I tagged along behind Chris Ralph and Tom Ripley, two experienced Hardrock runners from the state of Washington. Tom was having stomach problems of

26

his own, and we kept stopping so he could throw up. This slowed me down, but they knew the course so I didn't want to leave them. To shorten a long story I became discouraged going over Handies Peak, the course high point at 14,048 feet. Runners were supposed to climb all the way to the top of Handies where a punch had been placed to make a mark on our race numbers to prove we had been there. I had moved ahead of my two companions and was alone looking for Handies Peak. Frustrated because I didn't know where it was I just left the trail and started climbing up a likely looking rock glacier that turned out not to be Handies. The steep slope was endless and I never reached the top. Thoroughly exhausted, I returned to the trail, didn't bother to make the Handies climb when I got there, didn't punch my number, and eventually wound up dropping out of the race at Grouse Gulch.

That year it took me 18 hours to travel 42 miles. Wheezing and gasping when I returned to the motel, the only position where I could breathe comfortably was lying on the floor and arching my back.

When my lungs returned to normal I croaked to my son, "Steve, this race makes Leadville look like a fun run." Other Hardrock runners kept repeating the word "scope." Everything at Hardrock is on a larger scale than any other 100 mile trail race. The mountains are higher, the slopes are steeper, and the race takes longer to complete. The only thing that isn't bigger is the number of runners, which is kept purposely small for logistical reasons.

Sleeping on the floor that night I had an intensely erotic dream, a sign that I had been seduced by the mystical San Juans. Like Ulli Kamm, I had fallen hopelessly in love with everything about the Hardrock 100 race.

Legendary mountain runner and 1996 Hardrock 100 Winner, Rick Trujillo. Photo by Bob Boeder

Ulli Kamm receiving his 5th finishers award from RD Dale Garland. Photo by Judy Esser

In 1996, Rick Trujillo finally won Hardrock in 30:44 shepherded by his pacer, Ricky Denesik. Mark Hartell from Chester, England, running alone, nearly caught the two Ricks completing the course in 30:54. Betsy Kalmeyer was first woman in 40:43. Joel Zucker finished with ten minutes to spare. In his fourth attempt to conquer the Hardrock, Richard Senelly made a mad dash to cross the finish line with five seconds to spare. Suzi completed the course but she took five minutes and five seconds too long so race management established the tradition of listing those who exceed the 48-hour limit as unofficial finishers with an asterisk. Since I failed to reach even the halfway point, I viewed those who had finished as super humans, people who had been touched with radiance. For me they were gods of Olympus existing in a state of heightened strength and sentience that set them apart from ordinary folk. Filled with envy for their accomplishments, I promptly signed up for the next year's run.

After returning to North Carolina I registered for a 10K race in Mullins, South Carolina, directed by Franklin Mason. The course was flat and I thought that since I was in great shape from Hardrock I would record a fast time. I was shocked when I crossed the finish line in 46:24, four minutes slower than I usually ran 6.2 miles. Irate that the course was obviously too long, I asked other runners if their times were slower than normal and they said no. In subsequent races my leg speed was poor. Suspecting that running at altitude had ruined me for life, I called David Horton on the telephone.

"Hey, David, has running Hardrock affected your leg speed, made you slower than before?" I asked.

"Not that I've noticed. Why?" he replied.

"Because I've slowed considerably since I came back from Silverton, and I wondered if it was the altitude."

"Must be the years catching up with you. Happens to everybody. You only ran 40 miles at Hardrock. That's not enough to injure you permanently. Running in the San Juans and slowing down at the same time was just a coincidence."

"So in the future when I run Hardrock I'll not only have to contend with the terrain and the altitude, but with my aging process as well." I mused.

Hanging up the phone I wondered how much time I had left before I would no longer be able to achieve the cutoff times at trail ultras. Inhabiting a decaying body is like becoming a citizen of a foreign country. Habits change. Things are done differently. Confident strides become sudden stumbles. One's reach no longer exceeds one's grasp.

In 1997, I again remained in Fayetteville to direct my 10K on July 4 (it's a fund raiser for a charity supported by my church) then flew out to Denver and drove down to Silverton. After checking into the Triangle Motel (this time a single room on the ground floor) I only had a week to get acclimated and I was doing the race alone with neither crew nor pacer. On race day too much snow in the high country slowed me to a glacial pace. Defeated by the course, I dropped out in Ouray at the 43 mile point, matching my mileage of 1996 in the same amount of time. Making my DNF a little easier to swallow was the fact that I rode back to Silverton in the same vehicle with Julie Westland-Litus, a four time Hardrock finisher who had also dropped out.

Conversation on that ride back to the motel was minimal. Julie said she didn't care if she ever came back to enter the race again. And someone got a weak laugh by remarking, "This race makes all the other 100 milers look like Mother Theresa's picnic."

In 1997, Mark Hartell returned to Silverton bringing his UK buddy, Mark McDermott, and together, wearing fellrunner's shoes, they toured the course in 30:33 to tie for first place. Laura Vaughan, at that time the Wasatch Front 100 Mile course record holder, set a new woman's Hardrock record in 37:22. Suzi Thibeault redeemed herself by finishing the race in a respectable 46:45. Joel Zucker recorded his second consecutive Hardrock finish in 47:50, the identical time of his '96 finish, coming in last to win the Caboose Award. Ulli Kamm and Randy Rhodes became the first five-time finishers of the race. Snow, wind and freezing conditions on Engineers Pass and Handies Peak made 1997 the most difficult year as far as weather goes.

At the awards ceremony a song by the Little River Band kept going through my mind: "Have you heard about the lonesome loser. Beaten by the queen of hearts every time." Hardrock had become my queen of hearts. Thoroughly intoxicated, I thought about her every day, but she wouldn't let me go all the way.

The tendency of memory is to simplify, to deny ambiguity, and to dilute the failures of the past. Needless to say, I was one of the first to sign up for the 1998 Hardrock run. When they received my check race officials must have said, "This guy keeps sending in his application and DNFing. He's like a turd that won't flush."

I had the "wrong stuff" for two years in a row, but vowed to do it differently in '98. I had finally learned my lesson so I arranged for someone to take over my 10K race directing duties and flew out to Colorado two weeks ahead of time. My friends, Judy and Walt Esser, live in Cary, North Carolina, during the winter, but have a condo in Frisco, Colorado, where they spend part of the summer. When the Essers asked me if I was going to try Hardrock again in '98 and I replied, "Does Dolly Parton sleep on her back?" they volunteered to crew for me. I was ready to rock and roll.

After checking into my usual room at the Triangle, I tracked down Charlie Thorn and arranged to help him, John Cappis, and other early bird Hardrockers mark the course. Actually, I enjoyed course marking much more than the race. I wasn't under pressure to reach an aid station before a cutoff time so I adopted a leisurely pace, visited with the other runners, and stopped often to admire the marvelous scenery.

At the pre-race briefing, race director, Dale Garland, announced a Hardrock Jeff Foxworthy contest. Runners were supposed to submit endings to the sentence that began, "You know you're a Hardrock runner if..." My contribution was "...your shins look like they were run over by a power

31

mower." The winner of the contest was John Demorest with "…you need Viagra because every muscle in your body is stiff except one."

On race day Friday morning, it was pouring down rain so I stayed in Walt's Jeep Cherokee until 5:58 a.m., two minutes before the race started. I had a good feeling about the '98 event. An inner voice told me I was trained and acclimated and would do well. The rain stopped and Friday turned into a beautiful day. I moved smoothly through the first 30 miles of the counterclockwise route to the Sherman aid station, but Charlie Thorn had discovered a new route to Handies Peak called "Upchuck Ridge" and this climb was so impossibly steep that it absolutely destroyed me. After I descended from Handies into American Basin, the ensuing climb to American-Grouse Pass through difficult snowfields further smashed any appetite I had for continuing the race.

Arriving at Grouse Gulch at 11:00 p.m., I found Walt Esser ready to pace me to Ouray. Walt was entered in the Leadville 100 in August so I decided to stay in the race in order to give him some experience in nighttime running. In fact, I wasn't running at this point, I was walking rather slowly intending to drop out when we reached Ouray. At 3:00 a.m. while shambling half asleep down the Bear Creek Trail feeling sorry for myself, I stepped off the trail sending my left leg into space. Not especially wanting to spiral several hundred feet into Bear Creek Canyon, I threw all my weight on my right leg and fell on the trail instead, severely spraining my right ankle in the process.

This accident grimly sustained my decision to drop out of the race since there was no way on a hurting ankle I could motor up the steep scree slopes that awaited me, but I still had to hobble three miles to the aid station. Along the way my intestines rebelled and I was struck by diarrhea. This is where I learned how to squat on one leg with painful stomach cramps while relieving myself. After a half dozen episodes it felt like a red hot silver dollar was permanently imbedded in my rectum.

In 1998, Ricky Denesik of Telluride won the race in 30:12, paced by Rick Trujillo, returning the favor from 1996. David Horton was second, just 15 minutes behind Denesik. Eliza MacLean of Mebane, North Carolina, finished first woman in 40:57. Eliza crossed the finish line alongside Steve Simmons, of West Virginia, who had completed Western States just two weeks prior to Hardrock. The Western States-Hardrock double finish in the same year is one of the most difficult achievements in 100 mile trail ultrarunning. Besides Steve, only a few have done it–Martyn Greaves, twice in '93 and '94; Carl Yates in '93 when he was 65 years old; Bert Meyer in '94; Lee Schmidt in '94; Scott Mills in '96; and Gordon Hardman in '98.

By the time I dropped out at Ouray, Joel Zucker was six miles ahead of me. At around 8:00 a.m. Saturday, as he was starting the climb to Virginius Pass, he was struck by a severe headache. The pain ebbed on his final ascent to the pass, but came back so strong on the descent into Telluride that he had to stop. At the Telluride aid station, he took some aspirin. His pacer, Brian Scott, and run director, John Cappis, tried to convince Joel to lie down and rest in order to get the headache under control. Joel knew that taking extra time at an aid station would ruin his chances of finishing, so he refused to rest and endured the last 30 miles of the Hardrock course which took him over 20 hours with a splitting headache. Joel made one of his patented screaming yelling finishes in 47:37, the fastest of his three Hardrock completions, in 37th place out of 38.

At the awards ceremony on Sunday morning, Joel basked in the warm congratulations of well wishers, telling Steve Pattillo in his usual stutter, "S-S-S-Steve, I can't believe I'm th-th-three for th-th-three in the Hardrock."

On Monday morning Brian Scott; his wife, Sara; and their two children, Luke and Anna, collected Joel at Charlie Thorn's house for the ride back to the airport in Albuquerque. Joel announced he was "fully recovered from the race." He rode in the back seat of Brian's truck, goofing around with the kids, who called him Uncle Joel. They drove through Durango and stopped for lunch in Pagosa Springs where Joel ate three enchiladas and half of Anna's bean burrito. After lunch he fell asleep.

Joel Zucker with his pals, Congo and Bob. Photo by Gail Wood

On the remote section of New Mexico Highway 84 from Chama to Abiquiu, Joel took two sharp breaths in his sleep. The Scotts knew something was wrong and yelled at him to wake up but received no response. Brian pulled his vehicle over to the side of the road and checked Joel's neck for a pulse, but there was none. He hauled Joel out of the truck onto the dirt shoulder and began CPR. Sara was waving down passing cars and a state trooper stopped. After five minutes Joel's pulse came back and he regained partial consciousness. The trooper told Brian to start talking to Joel about something he had done recently so Brian told Joel he still needed to finish Hardrock. Upon hearing this news Joel opened his eyes and tried to sit up. Brian asked Joel if he had ever had a seizure before. Joel looked Brian in the eye and whispered, "No." Joel was able to move both his arms, but he started to fade, so Brian asked him to repeat the names of the Hardrock aid stations back to him as he said them. Joel did this with slurred speech.

The state trooper had radioed for an ambulance. Just as it arrived from Espanola, Joel lost his pulse and he stopped breathing. The EMT crew took over, restored his pulse and loaded him in the ambulance. Two people worked on Joel during the 30 minute drive to the hospital at Espanola. He was unresponsive. Riding in the front seat, Brian yelled at Joel, trying to reach him but to no avail. Joel was gone, but efforts to revive him continued.

At the Espanola hospital Joel's pulse was restored and arrangements were made to airlift him to Albuquerque. Joel's mother, Lynne, in New Paltz, New York, was informed of the situation as were Carolyn Erdman in Silverton and Charlie Thorn and Andi Kron in Los Alamos. As Joel's helicopter lifted off, a rainbow appeared in the sky in front of him. Brian and Luke drove to the hospital in Albuquerque where they found Joel lying in a bed hooked up to a life support system. His strong heart was beating on its own, but he needed a ventilator to breathe for him. Brian spent some time alone with Joel talking to him and touching him, but there was no response.

On Tuesday morning Brian was in Joel's room when the doctor told him Joel was not going to wake up. Brian brought

Luke in to say good-bye. The doctors were performing their final series of neurological tests. Joel was confirmed brain dead. Andi and Charlie arrived at the hospital along with Steve Pattillo and his wife, Peg, in time to say their good-byes. The cause of Joel's death was brain bleed, cerebral hemorrhage. He had high blood pressure but refused to take medication for it. Joel's mother requested that his organs be donated then his body was cremated. Half his ashes were sprinkled in Fall Creek near Ithaca, New York, by his friend, Gail Wood, and half would be placed beneath his plaque on Grant Swamp Pass, Joel's favorite place on the Hardrock course.

Did the extreme exertion at high altitude at the Hardrock race cause Joel's brain bleed? Except for a few events like the Western States 100 where medical checks are overdone, most trail ultra races, and Hardrock in particular, emphasize the individual's personal responsibility for his or her preparation for the event and safety during the race. The race application informs people that this is a "post graduate" run. Novice runners are not accepted. Those who choose Hardrock for their first 100 miler are discouraged. Qualifying standards for the race are as follows:

1.) Started any previous Hardrock (and therefore ran at least part of the course);

2.) Completion of the "Grand Slam of Ultrarunning" (this means finishing the Old Dominion, Western States, Leadville, and Wasatch Front 100 milers in one summer);

3.) Completion of any one of the following: Wasatch Front, Leadville, Angeles Crest, Western States, Eagle, or Massanutten 100 milers within the last 4 years.

Foreign candidates who have not had a chance to run any of the U.S. 100 milers must submit an account of their ultra/mountain running experience that convinces the select committee that they are prepared for the run.

The application form requests medical information including a list of regular medications that should be noted by the medical director, Dr. Lou Winkler. The Hardrock Runners

Manual suggests medical hints for runners and crew members about what to do in case of injury or loss of consciousness. This advice boils down to keeping the person warm and informing the volunteers at the nearest aid station. Each aid station is equipped with a first aid kit and is hooked up with race headquarters via ham radio.

At the check-in before the race, all runners are issued a Colorado Hiking Certificate. This certificate is like a search and rescue insurance policy because it entitles the holder to be rescued at no charge by the county search and rescue team should that become necessary. Pacers and crew members are urged to buy Hiking Certificates. Also, at the check-in, runners undergo a rudimentary medical exam by an EMT or a physician that is limited to measurement of their pulse and blood pressure rates. The pulse rate and any allergies or medications being taken are written along with the runner's name and number on a hospital bracelet that is attached to the runner's arm.

In Joel's case, run management was well aware of his medical problem. At the 1997 race his blood pressure measured 240/160 and medical personnel asked that he be tested again to ascertain that they had not made a mistake. He made no secret of the fact that he did not take medication for his condition. Should he have been permitted to run the race? At the 1998 check-in his top blood pressure number was 160. He was 44 years old, stood 5'3" tall, weighed 132 lbs., and was in excellent physical condition. His history of injuries included six stress fractures of his left tibia, chronic soreness in his right hamstring, tendinitis in his left knee, one leg longer than the other, and scoliosis (curvature of the spine) which made him tilt when he ran. Joel had been running for 22 years averaging 60 miles per week. In 1993, with eighty-five marathons under his belt, he began entering ultras. Besides two Hardrocks, he had completed six other hundred milers.

Should Joel have been pulled from the race at the Telluride aid station? For medical professionals, when someone who suffers from high blood pressure experiences an intense headache, a red flag goes up. John Cappis was the top race official at Telluride and was informed of Joel's headache. It was his call to pull Joel or to let him continue. John works for the Department of Energy in Los Alamos. A cautious, conservative bureaucrat, he is also an experienced ultrarunner who has been part of the Hardrock management team from the race's inception and finished Hardrock in 1992. Telluride is his hometown. His mother was the town postmaster and his parents still live there. He decided to let Joel continue.

When a runner is injured or having some problem but stays in the race, aid station volunteers should inform the race director and medical personnel as well as aid stations down the line so they can monitor that individual's progress. There is no evidence that this was done in Joel's case. Since Joel's history of high blood pressure was known to race management, the medical director should have talked to him about his situation when he finished the race. There is no evidence that this was done either. When Joel left the finish area he was on his own.

Most of the time when ultrarunners have had enough or are injured or clearly unfit to continue, they realize it and pull themselves out of races on their own volition or after discussing their situations with race officials. Some ultrarunners have more of their manhood involved in finishing a race than do others. Joel was one of these. For Joel, as for many of the Hardrock runners, this event is the highlight of the year. It's the only race that matters. Everything else is training for Hardrock. Being a Hardrock finisher meant everything to Joel, who described himself as being a member of a "special group" consisting of "short, Jewish, tattooed, ultrarunning librarians."

Ultrarunning and dogs were Joel's life. He had a poor relationship with his father all his life and as an adult held a series of college librarian jobs for which he was vastly overqualified. He never married and didn't want children. He was fun loving and gregarious, but he felt most at ease with other people when they were at arm's length. Hence, his zeal for computer relationships where his stutter did not get in the way and where emotions are not as powerful and complicated as they are when dealing face to face with other human beings.

Joel was intensely proud of being one of the handful of ultrarunners who have recorded multiple Hardrock finishes. His manhood was completely entwined in the fabric of this race. For Joel, to quit, to drop out of Hardrock was unthinkable. It's no exaggeration to say that in order to persuade him to drop out voluntarily you would have to shoot him. To withdraw Joel from the race against his wishes when he clearly wanted to continue and appeared physically able to continue despite his headache was beyond John Cappis' ken. So Joel stayed in the race.

What would have happened had he been withdrawn at Telluride? Probably a night spent in a hospital undergoing a few tests. Could doctors have prevented the hemorrhage that killed him? No. A pressure bleed is like a stroke. Once you bleed there is little that can be done. Joel spent his final days surrounded by a loving and supportive community of close friends who shared their lives with him. When he died he was at his peak, on top of the world, flying high from another Hardrock finish. There are worse ways to go.   Joel was the person responsible for his own health. He decided whether or not to take medication for his high blood pressure. He chose not to.

In the urbanized Western world where medical care is easily accessible, most individuals live at least into their 70's. People are not accustomed to death. The passing of a loved one hits them like a thunderbolt and they have trouble coping with their sadness and sense of loss. In places like Africa where medical care is minimal, child mortality rates are high, and disease is rampant, death is common. People mourn their lost relatives, but death is accepted as part of life. The dead are believed to affect the lives of the living in many ways, so they are not forgotten. They must be placated or they can cause problems for the living. The dead, the living, and the yet-to-be-born are all part of a continuum.

In September, like a tongue returning compulsively to a broken tooth, I mail in my $150.00 for the 1999 race. My specific training for the upcoming Hardrock 100 starts in October, 1998, when my right ankle finally feels normal. While running on some trails in Virginia with Web Loudat, an All American steeplechase runner at the University of New Mexico in the 1960's, he informs me that while I am technically proficient running steep stony downhills I need to improve my uphill technique. When running uphill I don't maintain an even speed. I tend to go in spurts, running hard for a few minutes then dropping back before surging again. This is because my heart can't keep up with my leg speed/muscle work rate. To sustain an all out uphill effort I must maintain a high heart beat in order to keep blood flowing steadily to my muscles. To improve, I need to do tempo runs over an extended period of time–like two years.

Web and I begin weekly speed work running all out for one mile on a hilly gravel road, taking a two minute breather, then turning around and running as hard as we can back to where we started. When he was forty years old Web was one of the top master milers in the world, running a 4:19 to win the Wanamaker Mile race and beating Frank Shorter, Barry Brown, and all the top guys in the process. He is in his early fifties now and due to a bad knee is basically running on one leg, but he has no trouble keeping up with me as I crank out my miles,–usually 7:13 for the first one then around 7:25 for the second. I wonder if I'll ever get any faster. Then one day in January I break through and run 7:00 for the first mile then 7:13 for the second. Jubilation.

Meanwhile I have been entering races. On October 17, I finish the Mountain Masochist 50 Mile Trail Race in 11:45, 15 minutes under the maximum time allowed. Directed by David Horton, this race is a few miles longer than 50, but inexact mileage is common in these events and I don't mind.

It's the fifth time I have completed the Mountain Masochist, and I had to push it in order get in under 12 hours. I'd like to go for ten Mountain Masochist 50 finishes, but don't know if I will be able to maintain enough leg speed in the future. Another runner and I teamed up to run the last 15 miles together. I led the way and he fed off me, but the arrangement was reciprocal because without him pushing me I would not have run as fast. The Mountain Masochist 50 miler acts as an annual litmus test for me. If I can complete the race in under 12 hours, then I still consider myself a legitimate trail ultrarunner. If I fail then I'd better find another sport. The 1998 race was an eye opener. Fifteen minutes to spare is getting too close to the cutoff. I decide to make some changes in my life designed to make me a better runner. The main change is to lose ten pounds. At six feet tall I weigh 180 pounds, which is too much to haul for 50 miles. Getting enough exercise isn't the problem. I'm running 60 miles a week, so the day after the Mountain Masochist I take a hard look at my diet. Low fat is the name of the new game. No more ice cream, no more pastry, good-bye donuts, farewell mixed nuts. I've always eaten a no junk food, healthy diet with plenty of fruits and vegetables, but I tended to pamper myself with between meal snacks and before bed "you've been a good boy today" treats. No more. The only snacks I'm allowing myself are the no fat ones that taste like cardboard. I also make some new equipment purchases designed to help me survive Hardrock.

In November I buy a pair of fleece running pants, a new gore-tex running suit to keep me warm at night above the tree line, and an Ultimate Sport Vest. The Sport Vest features a camelback that holds 80 ounces of fluids and three pockets in front sewn onto a mesh vest that slips over my head like a singlet. Adjustable straps on both sides make it easy to pull on and off, and lightweight pants or a jacket can be carried in a mesh net on the back. It takes me a few tries to figure out how to bite down on the mouthpiece and suck out fluids while running uphill, but the Sport Vest doesn't bounce like my fanny pack did, and I can carry more fluids, which is important for Hardrock since the aid stations are so far apart. I have drunk water from streams on the course during the race, and it was the sweetest, coldest water I have ever had, but race management doesn't recommend drinking from the streams since contracting giardia is always a possibility. The stomach distress caused by giardia isn't fun. The upside is that it doesn't affect a person until two weeks after entering your system so you won't have any problems during the race.

On November 7, I enter the Pine Mountain Trail Run in Georgia directed by ultrarunner Jim Musselman and complete the 46 miles in 11:16.

On December 12, I run the Rocket City Marathon in Huntsville, Alabama, and am pleased with my 3:35 time on a cold wet day. Driving home through the mountains of western North Carolina, I meet my friend, Sarah Lowell, for a trail run. Sarah once held the women's course record at the Umstead 100 and is a three time finisher and course record holder at the Coldfoot 100 in Alaska. She mentions an adventure race scheduled for March at the Nantahala Outdoor Center (NOC) near Bryson City, North Carolina, and I immediately decide to enter. It's a three-person team event requiring rafting, canoeing, mountain biking, and orienteering, so I ask Sarah to join me on a team. She doesn't want to commit herself at this point. I tell her I'm going to pester her until she agrees to do the race.

After completing Rocket City I journey to Charleston, West Virginia, the next weekend to run the Snowflake 50K, organized by Dennis Hamrick and Mickey Jones in Kanawa State Forest. I come in 10th overall in the Snowflake race in 5:28.

On January 1, I do a Fat Ass 50K organized by Walt Esser in Umstead State Park. The rest of January is consumed with planning for the Uwharrie Trail 40, 20, and 8 Mile Adventure Runs on February 6-7. A total of 368 people finish the three races, combined. It's a relief when the weekend is over and I can refocus on training for Hardrock.

In late February I spend a weekend trashing my quads running the Appalachian Trail in preparation for the NOC Adventure Race. Tom Gamblin, an ultrarunner who has recorded 2:45 marathons and finished the Raid Gauloise adventure race in Lesotho a few years ago, has agreed to team up with me, but Sarah is giving me a hard time. Having a female as the third team member is mandatory. A half dozen women, all experienced trail ultrarunners, turn me down for various reasons. I prefer recruiting women who are ultrarunners because I know they won't quit when the going gets difficult. I keep bugging Sarah. Besides being an outstanding trail runner she's an excellent mountain biker and does lots of kayaking on the Nantahala River where part of the race will be held, but she lacks confidence in her canoeing and rafting skills. I tell her that each of us has strengths and weaknesses and where one of us is weak the other team members will help out. Finally, after setting the women's record at the Iditasport 100 Miler in Alaska, she agrees to join Tom and me on our team, but she forgets to tell me she suffered a broken wrist in Alaska.

On March 6, the Saturday before the NOC race, I enter the Holiday Lake 50K race directed by David Horton near Appomatox, Virginia. My weight-reducing plan is working and I'm down to 170 lbs., but my time of 6:12 on a cold, wet day is slow. I probably should have stayed home and rested for the adventure race, but I've always had more guts than brains.

On March 13, Sarah (with her wrist healed but still in a cast), Tom, and I and 39 other teams start the adventure race by rafting down the Nantahala River in a snowstorm. After that we paddle a canoe on Lake Fontana for five hours. When we arrive at the transition area and roll out of the canoe, my feet are so frozen I have to pound them on the ground for several minutes to restore circulation so I can stand up. A six hour mountain bike ride follows, first on the Tsali trail then on some very steep downhill jeep roads and a bushwhacking section on a trail. At the end of the bike phase we are in eleventh place, but during the night cold, wind, sleet, snow and rain cause navigation problems on the unmarked course, so we wind up finishing in eighteenth place after 26 hours. On Monday my quads are thoroughly trashed, my feet are so swollen I can barely walk, and I take a sick day off from work. Except for the unmarked course I enjoyed my first adventure race. It was good training for Hardrock.

While I'm doing the adventure race, my speed workout buddy, Web, is in Colorado undergoing a knee operation. The doctor discovers that running on hard surfaces for many years has destroyed the cartilage in Web's knee. He patches it up as best he can, but informs Web that if he continues running he will eventually become crippled. This is the news every obsessive runner dreads-the end of the road. Most of us would be devastated. Web is resilient. Instead of feeling sorry for himself he undergoes painful daily rehabilitation exercises on his knee and swims lap after lap in the pool. It's like he's swimming for his life. Without Web's encouraging presence I lose interest in speed workouts.

On March 27, I finish tenth overall (out of 26 starters) in 8:52 at the Gator Gallop 50 miler held on the shores of Lake Waccamaw, North Carolina. I finished this race running strong. The start was a different story. Shortly after the gun went off, the mountain of spaghetti and the four pieces of chocolate cake I had consumed at the pre-race carbo loading dinner the previous evening all arrived at my backdoor at once. The problem was that the nearest toilet was at the Methodist Church two miles distant. I searched diligently alongside the road for anything resembling a plug – a stone, a corncob, a large wad of cardboard – without success. Soon I was reaching back with my hand clutching at my cheeks trying to prevent a serious breech of the levee.

Thankfully, I reached the church with only a minor browning of my running shorts. Upon departing from the squat station, I carried on with the race only to encounter a local woman giving her large red mixed breed his morning exercise unleashed. I tried to sneak past the two, but the mutt caught a whiff of my shorts and fell in love. Making a beeline for me from behind, he executed a perfect chop block sending me sprawling to the pavement at the feet of his mistress. Snarling something about "keeping your damn dog on a leash," I leaped up and kept running, and the dog returned to his pee and sniff game.

Two weeks later, on April 10, I run half the Umstead 100 miler in 10:54. I feel like a wimp doing 50 miles at Umstead instead of the Full Monty, but Hardrock is my main focus and a 50 mile training run is preferable at this point rather than a 100 mile total trashing of my mind and body. The past two years I have completed both the Umstead 100 in April and the Massanutten 100 mile trail race in May as training runs for Hardrock. I suspect that after these two 100 mile races I may have gone into the Colorado event still physically tired or at least with lower mental energy than normal, so this year I'm saving myself for Hardrock.

It's a sunny breezy day at Umstead and I amuse myself by unofficially disqualifying other runners for various transgressions. Joe Schlereth sets a new sub-seven hour record for 50 miles and I disqualify him twice for running too fast. Another guy gets sent off on two counts – passing me and running uphill. I'm getting ready to can a runner for being too slow when he dumps me first for noisy breathing. I run a few miles with Dixie Madsen of San Diego, California. Dixie is a nurse and she tells me that one of the side effects of taking high bood pressure medicine is impotence, which might explain why Joel didn't want to take his pills. Joel was a two-time Umstead finisher. Race director, Blake Norwood, talks about him at the pre-race briefing. This year someone is wearing his 1998 Umstead number 7 as a remembrance.

Normally I run six miles on weekdays during my lunch hour then do twenty on Saturday and ten on Sunday for a total of 60 miles per week, not counting races. On April 20, I increase my weekly mileage to 80 by adding a second run of ten miles after work on Tuesdays and Thursdays. Good training for Hardrock.

On April 24, I enter the 7-mile Bent Creek Trail Race organized by Anne Riddle and Geoff Sidoli, near Asheville, North Carolina. The older I get and the more I run, the tighter my muscles become. Despite lots of stretching chronic soreness in my left hamstring muscle forces me to start slowly. After a couple of miles my leg loosens up and I start to roll. About a half mile from the finish line I pass a thirteen year old girl on an uphill then open it up for a kamikaze downhill dash to the tape. Apparently, the girl doesn't like being beaten by an older gentleman. Half way down the hill I hear her breathing right behind me. We're in an all out guts on the trail death duel. Just before the finish line as I feel her passing me I lose control of my left arm which flies out in a clothesline maneuver. She is so short she runs right under my outstretched arm and pipps me by a hair. In the finishing chute I reach out playfully as if to strangle her, drawing appreciative laughter from onlookers. As penance, in the afternoon I hike 14 miles on the Appalachian Trail.

On a cold, wet, and windy Saturday morning, May 1, I run the 20 mile Longstreet Race on Fort Bragg finishing in 2:51, good for second in my age group, but a far cry from the 2:24 I ran in 1990 when I was the master's winner in this race. This is my home course, the hilly 20 miles I have covered on many a Saturday morning during the past 16 years. Most of the other runners are young soldiers. As always, they start out like gang busters, but run out of gas past the half way point, and I wind up passing a lot of them as they walk the final miles.

Although they are faster I'm in better physical condition than men who are 30 years younger. Like a mechanic fretting over a vintage automobile, I spend a lot of time on the care and maintenance of my body: eating the right foods, getting my rest, taking extra vitamins. To reduce the soreness in my hamstring, I'm stretching a lot and applying analgesic ointment to the back of my leg. I've always stretched before every training run, but now I stretch both before and after and do specific hamstring stretches. If I stop stretching for a week, I tighten up so badly I can barely get out of my chair. South African physician Tim Noakes, author of the *Lore of Running*, says that runners can cure most of their injuries themselves if they stop and analyze what is happening and why, then take steps to prevent whatever is causing the problem.

Instead of tackling the Massanutten 100 miler this year, I've signed up for the Ice Age 50 Mile National Championship Trail Race on May 8 in Kettle Moraine State Park near Whitewater, Wisconsin. On a cool but humid day I start out well, knocking off the first 18 miles in just over three hours, but then I become dehydrated, slow to a crawl, and am passed by many, many runners. Finally, after restoring my fluids, I get back on track, start "movin' and groovin'" in the last ten miles, and finish strong in 11:09. Somebody tells me there are 75 hills in this race. None of them are major league long climbs, but they keep coming. Local runners slow for the downhills which I pound, but then they eat me up on the uphills. Carolyn Erdman completes the race, her tenth Ice Age 50 finish. Eric Clifton, now 40 years old, wins the race and becomes the national 50-mile trail champion for 1999. Eric is my favorite trail runner. He makes every race he enters exciting because he always goes out hard. He has been criticized for not tailoring his race tactics to suit the course, but he ignores nitpickers. If you want to race and win, Eric will make you work hard to beat him.

At Ice Age I meet Frank Bozanich for the first time. Frank is a legendary guy, a top long distance runner in the 1970's who worked as a policeman among the Inuit people in Alaska for years before joining the force in Reno, Nevada. At 55, Frank still runs marathons under three hours and 50-mile trail races under eight hours.

Typically, after crossing the finish line at Ice Age, I am overcome by emotions briefly then the endorphins kick in and

I feel terrific. After the race I drive over to Minneapolis where I celebrate Mother's Day with my Ma, who is 90 years old. Even though my three 50 mile races this spring each took progressively more time to complete I was running well at the finish in all of them. This is a good sign, more "training for Hardrock," because I will have to be strong in the last 20 miles in order to finish in under 48 hours.

At this point, my usual 20 mile Saturday morning training run on Longstreet is only maintaining my fitness. I'm not stressing anything, not improving, so the weekend after Ice Age I head for the Uwharrie Trail to do 24 miles on a cool, green, sunny day. The first 12 miles feel strong and confident, but then the fatigue from last Saturday's 50 miles of exertion sets in and I finish slow. About a half mile from the parking lot, I get a thrill when I run past a five foot long black snake with yellow bands around it that has just crossed the trail. It's tail is rattling softly.

Twenty feet down the trail I stop, turn around, and watch the snake. It's just sitting there, waiting to see what I'm going to do. I haven't seen one of these snakes before. It's not a diamondback–wrong coloring; it's not a cottonmouth–it's too far west; it must be a timber rattler. I love seeing these snakes in the woods. They are beautiful and only defend themselves when provoked. They just want to be left alone to eat rodents and lie in the sun.

The next weekend, May 22-23, my search for more challenging training runs takes me to Doughton Park on the Blue Ridge Parkway, between Roaring Gap and Laurel Springs, North Carolina. Walt Esser and Joe Schlereth join me, and we stay at Blake Norwood's cabin on the New River. Blake has plantar fascitis, inflammation of the plantar fascia tendon on the bottom of his foot, so he rides his bike on the parkway while the rest of us run the trails. The course is 27 miles and includes some of the longest steepest climbs on the east coast. It was one of Eric Clifton's favorite training areas when he lived in North Carolina.

Early Saturday morning we leave our vehicles in a parking lot on the parkway, run 2.8 miles steeply down Bluff Ridge Trail to Grassy Gap Road, follow the road a mile and a half east, climb the 4.8 mile Cedar Ridge Trail up to Brinegar's Cabin on the parkway where there is a water fountain, turn around and run back down the Cedar Ridge Trail to Grassy Gap Road, turn west and stay on the road for 6 ½ miles all the way up to the parkway where we have stashed some water and sandwiches, eat, then go back down Grassy Gap Road and end our day by climbing back up the Bluff Ridge Trail to our vehicles. Is that clear? Along the way I start referring to Bluff Ridge Trail in my mind as *No Mas* Trail. Once I reach the top I am finished for the day.

The three of us get separated along the way with Joe leading, Walt in the middle, and me bringing up the rear. Walt and I hike the uphills while Joe runs the entire course, "grinding" up the Grassy Gap road. Walt and Joe are training for Western States. It will be Walt's first trip to the High Sierras while Joe is going for his tenth sub-24 hour finish at Western States. Most of the time he runs Western States in 19-20 hours. Joe is famous for recording 9000 training miles a year, averaging around 25 miles per day. He's an amazing athlete, absolutely determined to do well at Western States. He lives in Charlotte and has been running in the North Carolina heat wearing sweat clothes. Some people who wear rubber suits or sweat clothes and run in the summer overheat and end up hospitalized in a coma, but for Joe it's just another day at the office. Today he does the 27 mile course and throws in another 14 miles just for fun. I'm impressed. I've read about Joe and how he trains, but actually being there while he's doing it motivates me. Joe has been one of the best trail runners in the country for a long time, and he is working his butt off to stay on top.

The trails on the Blue Ridge are pretty this time of year with purple rhododendron, pink and white mountain laurel, and orange and yellow azaleas just starting to bloom. On

Sunday morning my quads are sore, but I join the others for a ten miler down and up Grassy Gap Road.

The following Saturday, Walt and I are back at Doughton Park for another 27-mile fun run. We're in no rush. The time spent on the trail is as important as the distance covered. It takes us about eight hours to complete the course. Along the way we flush a spotted fawn from its hiding place under a log and see wild turkeys and guinea fowl. I've been experimenting with different shoes trying out Nike Armas, Nike Humaras, and the new Montrail Vitesse. The Armas-regular lightweight running shoes-don't provide enough support on steep rocky trails, the trail oriented Humaras don't fit me right, but the Montrails-too clunky for road running-are working fine on these Blue Ridge mountain trails. My quads stand up to the pounding. That means I'm in good physical shape. The mental aspect will be paramount at Hardrock. I need to be confident and maintain my focus on finishing the race, not be defeated by temporary slow going in the high country. I must keep a positive attitude, not become discouraged when faced with unforeseen situations, and be prepared to suffer.

On the weekend of June 5-6, I crew for Harvey Hall at the Old Dominion 100 miler. Harvey helped me during my Grand Slam summer in 1994, and I am eternally indebted to him. I've paced a few times, but never crewed before. It's a good opportunity to catch up with friends I haven't seen for a couple of years. Crewing turns out to consist of hours of waiting interspersed with a few minutes of terror when Harvey arrives and I stress out in fear that I don't have what he wants or that I forgot something in my vehicle which is parked half a mile down the road. I avoid major screw-ups and Harv finishes in under 23 hours, so the venture is a success. I get in a 12-mile run and some sleep deprivation practice by staying up all night.

Helping Harvey at Old Dominion amounted to taking the weekend off from running which was fine because I needed the rest. This wasn't the case for several people who warmed up for Hardrock by running Old Dominion. Jim Musselman, Tom Green, John DeWalt, Kerry Trammell, and Leslie Hunt all finished OD while Rob Youngren DNFed at 75 miles and Dennis Herr retired at the half way point. Musselman and DeWalt came out of the race injured-Jim with tendenitis in his ankle and John with an ankle bruise and what looked like a broken middle toe on his right foot. Not a promising situation only five weeks before Hardrock.

David Horton was at Old Dominion helping some friends. He's not signed up for Hardrock this year because he is going to run the Vermont Long Trail from June 7-11 in an attempt to break Countney Campbell's 1998 record of 5 1/2 days for the 270 miles. David explains his success at Hardrock by saying, "I race better than I am." This refers to David's intense competitiveness and willingness to do whatever is necessary to win. I'll need some of Horton's desire to do well if I am going to finish Hardrock.

David Horton and Eric Clifton have been two of the best trail ultrarunners on the east coast for over fifteen years. Both have outgoing personalities and love to talk about races and race courses. Eric is the more flamboyant of the two with his trademark colorful tights and "go out hard" running style. Intensely religious, David is more of a come-from-behind tactical runner. Eric's speciality is speed while David does well on highly technical courses like Hardrock. They are friendly rivals, but the mutual kidding can get heavy handed.

On June 12 I return to Doughton Park for another 27-mile trail workout. Joe Schlereth is there for his 41-mile workout. In the past Joe suffered from plantar fascitis, but cured it by putting orthotics in his running shoes. Running together we catch a group of three horses and riders from behind. Horses have mainly straight ahead vision so when they hear something behind them, they lash out with their hooves. As we approach I call out a warning to the riders. They stop and position their mounts so they can see us when we pass. At the end of the day Joe and I wish each other well in our upcoming events.

Joe and I have been preparing for a year. We are on a mission to meet our goals and prove something to ourselves. Ultrarunning is like that. It's more than a hobby: it's practically a religion. We're about to set off on our annual pilgrimages-Joe to the Sierras in California, me to Colorado's Rockies-to join like-minded friends in a celebration of life. It's a gathering of the devout to revel in the spirit of the mountains, to seek wisdom and inspiration, to test ourselves once more-like Muslims to Mecca, Catholics to Rome, or Jews to Jerusalem's Wailing Wall.

Circling the San Juans every July at Hardrock bears a distant similarity to the Japanese Buddhist practice of *kaihogyo*, or mountain marathoning. John Stevens has written a book called *The Marathon Monks of Mount Hiei* which is one of Charlie Thorn's favorite books. The practice of mountain pilgrimages, of circling peaks regarded as sacred, existed in Chinese Buddhism and developed in Japan in the second half of the ninth and early tenth centuries. At first the pilgrimage was free style, but over the years buildings and shrines were established on Mount Hiei and other mountains; the manner of dress, basic routes, and procedures were codified. By 1571, the course was 40 kilometers (24.8 miles) and the full term was 700 days of running followed by a nine day fast.

Gyoja is a Japanese word for someone who is undergoing strict Buddhist training-an ascetic or spiritual athlete. Another translation is "one who is moving along the path of awakening." Novice monks must learn the course, prayers, rituals, and chants for each shrine. The Hiei uniform is pure white, made of cotton, and consists of a short kimono undershirt, pants, hand and leg covers, a long outer robe, and a priest's surplice. The cord of death with a sheathed knife is fastened around the monk's waist. White is the Buddhist color of death, and the *gyoja* is obliged to kill himself by hanging or stabbing if he fails to complete any part of the practice. He carries a small bag containing his prayer book, candle and matches, and his rosary. *Higasa*, the trademark elongated hat of the Hiei *gyoja*, is carried for the first 300 days of training. He wears straw sandals, which disintegrate easily in rain. Straw raincoats and paper lanterns to light the way are also carried except during storms when plastic raincoats and flashlights are permitted. The monk runs alone.

The five basic rules of kaihogyo are:

1.) Do not remove your hat or robe during a run.
2.) Stay on the course.
3.) Do not stop for rest or refreshment.
4.) Correctly perform all prayers and chants.
5.) Do not smoke or drink.

The runs start at 1:30 am. Two courses exist on Mount Hiei, one of 30 kilometers (18.6 miles) and the other of 40 kilometers. Both are demanding-full of stairs and steep slopes. Over 250 stations of worship are found on each course-Shinto and Buddhist temples and shrines, tombs, Buddha images, sacred groves, hills, stones, and peaks. Stops at the stations range from ten seconds to two minutes. The monk only sits down once on a bench for a two minute prayer to the emperor. The run is over between 7:30 and 9:00 a.m. Following a one hour prayer service, the monk eats lunch, rests for an hour, attends another service at 3:00 p.m., eats again at 6:00 p.m., then goes to bed at 8:00 or 9:00. Rise and shine is at midnight for an hour service followed by a couple of rice balls and some soup; then it's out the door for another run. This regimen is repeated for 100 days. Two-thirds of the way through the 100 days, the monk does a 54-kilometer (33.5 miles) run through Kyoto, stopping at numerous shrines. This takes 24 hours and he must do the marathon immediately after returning to Hiei.

A monk takes about 30 days to grow accustomed to the pounding. His most common physical problems are swollen legs, sore achilles tendons, and hip and back pains. By day 70 he is used to the schedule. After completing the 100 day term, the monk may apply for the 1000 day challenge over a period of seven years. The 1000 day challenge breaks down as follows:

Year 1 100 days   30 or 40 km/day depending on course, carry hat.

Year 2 100 days   30 or 40 km/day depending on course, carry hat.

Year 3 100 days   30 or 40 km/day depending on course, carry hat.

Year 4 200 days   30 or 40 km/day depending on course, wear hat starting on day 301.

Year 5 200 days   30 or 40 km/day depending on course, wooden staff permitted from day 501.

On day 700, start *doiri*-nine days without food, water, sleep or rest. Can result in death.

Year 6 100 days   60 kilometers/day (37.2 miles).

Year 7 100 days   84 kilometers/day (52.1 miles).

100 days   30 or 40 kilometers/day.

Total   1000 days 38,632 or 46,572 kilometers depending on which course is chosen.

A *gyoja* spends 7 ½ days of the nine day *doiri* sitting in the lotus position reciting a mantra to the Great Holy One, *Fudo Myo-o* over and over-100,000 times. Once every 24 hours, he gets up and walks out to a well and brings back a bucket of water that is offered to an image of *Fudo Myo-o*. Two monks sit with him to make sure he stays awake. Nausea begins on day two or three, hunger pangs cease by day four, by day five he is so dehydrated he is allowed to take a mouthful of water, rinse, and spit it out to prevent the sides of his mouth from adhering permanently. Defecation ceases on day three or four, but weak urination continues the entire time. The walk to the well peps him up. *Gyojas* claim to absorb water through their skin if it is raining. The hardest part is not going without food or water but staying awake and maintaining correct posture, especially keeping the head erect. During *doiri,* the senses, especially smell and hearing, are magnified. At the end of *doiri,* a special medicinal drink is given to revive the monk. He feels transparent, as if everything-good, bad and indifferent-has come out of him and he has achieved Enlightenment as a living Buddha. He sucks on ice and drinks only fluids for two weeks after *doiri* and sleeps only two or three hours per night.

In the sixth year the distance and the course difficulty increase, so it takes fourteen or fifteen hours to complete. Year seven brings the 100 days of 84 kilometer loops, the Great Marathon, which starts at 12:30 a.m. and takes sixteen to eighteen hours. The route goes through Kyoto and includes the red light district and 300 worship stations. The monk blesses all kinds of people during the Great Marathon. He is regarded as the incarnation of the great saint, *Fudo Myo-o*, capable of all kinds of miracles. Pushers gently assist the monk on straightaways during the Great Marathon. The monk doesn't get much sleep, but what he does get is deep and sound. During the Great Marathon helpers prepare the monk's meals and help him by directing traffic and washing his clothes.

Two or three years after completing the 1000 day marathon, a monk may choose to do the eight-day fire ceremony. This consists of fasting while sitting in front of a roaring blaze which is fed by tossing in up to 150,000 prayer sticks which people pay to have blessed. The fire ceremony practically mummifies the monk and is described as "like being roasted in hell." The purpose of this ritual is to consume all evil and purify the world. Forty-six monks have done the full 1000 day workout since 1885. Two did two full 1000 day terms, one committed suicide on day 2,500, and one did three terms though he didn't run every day of his third term. The oldest was 61 when he finished day 2000.

Beginning marathon monks train by doing manual labor and attending to senior marathon monks. They eat vegetarian meals-noodles, potatoes, tofu, rice gruel, seaweed-about 1450 calories per day, 500 less than dieticians say they should eat, but they don't lose weight. They develop the ability to catnap standing up and they run with rhythm, breath control and intense concentration. Marathon monks are similar to the *lung-gom-pa* runners of old Tibet, who reportedly could run non-stop for 48 hours and cover 200 miles per day.

Marathon monks are motivated by the desire to realize Buddhahood for themselves and for the sake of others. Their motto: "Learn through the eyes, practice with the feet." Their pilgrimage, carried out in silence on a remote and mystical mountain far from the noise and restlessness of the everyday world, is a search for Buddhist enlightenment. When this is achieved the monk becomes one with the mountain, flying along a path that is free of obstruction.

When Joel came to Silverton he ran a 13 mile course up and down Kendall Mountain every day in preparation for Hardrock. This was his *kaihogyo*, his mountain marathon training.

On Saturday, June 19, I fly from Fayetteville to Denver to commence the high altitude phase of my training. Judy and Walt Esser's condo in Frisco, my headquarters for the next two weeks, is at 9,097 feet. The Essers are in California preparing for Walt's attempt to run Western States. Afterwards they will drive to Silverton to crew for me at Hardrock. Entering the condo on Saturday evening I feel a burst of joy in my heart. I'm grateful to leave my normal life behind and to be surrounded by these mountains while I prepare for the ultimate test.

On Sunday morning I drive over to Leadville to attend a worship service at Good Shepherd Lutheran Church. The afternoon is spent running and hiking on the Turquoise Lake trail from Tabor Boat Landing to May Queen then on the Colorado Trail before retracing my steps to Tabor. Elapsed time: 5 hours.

Monday I stay in Frisco and run/hike the Meadows Creek Trail as far as I can in the direction of Eccles Pass before being stopped below the tree line by deep snow. With snow shoes and some way to mark my path I could have continued to the top of the pass, but it will be several weeks before the snow melts enough to reveal the trail. Retreating to the trail head, I do an out-and-back on the Lily Pad Lake Trail for a total of six hours of high altitude exercise.

I'm pleased with my acclimatization so far. I'm experiencing some lung tightness on steep uphills, but I'm having no trouble running the downhills, and I don't have a headache when I wake up in the morning. In 1993, the first year I came out to run in the Rockies, I couldn't take five quick steps forward without the blood pounding in my brain and my legs turning to cement. Now, after six summers of running at altitude, except for achy lungs, my body adapts well to the thin air. I can only imagine what it must have felt like for Joel to train up here with his high blood pressure.

Tuesday I hike Miners Creek Road out of Frisco then join Peaks Trail which takes me over to Breckenridge. Retracing my steps, I run through some light rain that produces a wonderfully piney scent in the woods. Total elapsed time: 6 hours.

On Wednesday, I take the Miners Creek Road once again, but when the road ends I continue on the Miners Creek Trail until four-foot deep snowdrifts at 11,000 feet put an end to my excursion. Returning to the road I repeat my Peaks Trail run of the day before over to Cucumber Creek and back; then I have the bright idea of hiking the Gold Hill Trail. This brings me to the trailhead on Highway 9 half way to Breckenridge, so I wind up running back to Frisco on the highway. Total exercise time for the day: 7 hours.

Each afternoon when I return to the condo I shower, eat, then take a nap. After my nap I write down some notes about my day's activities, eat supper, then watch a Rockies baseball game or one of the Womens World Cup soccer games. My daughter, Tisa, is a soccer player and I'm a big fan of the women's game.

Wednesday evening I telephone Roch Horton, a Frisco local who is signed up for Hardrock, and ask him to suggest some high country trails that are free of snow. Roch is very helpful. On Thursday, I take his advice and drive over to nearby Silverthorne to climb to the top of Ptarmigan Pass. This turns out to be a 5.5 mile uphill jaunt. Breaking out of treeline, I encounter a herd of 30 elk with a dozen calves. I approach to within 50 yards before they detect me and scamper into the trees for protection. A stiff wind sweeps the top of the climb at 12,490 feet, a bare, rounded knob on the Continental Divide. A ptarmigan is there to greet me. The pigeon-like bird stays on the ground as I chase after it. The views of the surrounding peaks and sailboats on Lake Dillon are terrific. The Ptarmigan Pass trail hasn't made me work hard enough, so after returning to Frisco I tackle the Mount Royal trail which is surprisingly steep and nasty. On Mount Royal I get in some rock scrambling and bushwhacking-good training for Hardrock. Total workout: 6 hours.

Early Friday morning I drive over to Loveland Pass (11,900 feet) where the prevailing westerly winds have blasted all the snow off the ridge tops and nearly carry me off as well. Just a hundred yards from where I park, I run into two shaggy-coated mountain goats who act like they own the place and are in no hurry to get out of my way. Eventually, after practicing following faint animal trails similar to the ones on the Hardrock course, I climb to the top of Mt. Sniktau (13,234 feet). Sitting down among the rocks recording my achievement on the Colorado Mountain Club ledger of summiteers, I feel something tugging at the pocket of my shorts. I look down and there's a small marmot trying to crawl into my pocket to steal my car keys. These marmots will do anything for a meal. Total time spent above Loveland Pass: 5 hours. Afterward I drive over to Fairplay, Colorado, for a late lunch.

On Saturday I drive over to Snow Mountain Ranch, a YMCA facility north of Winter Park, where I'm entered in the 20-Kilometer Snow Mountain Ranch trail race. The ranch is at 8,750 feet. There's nothing technical about the trail; it's just a rolling course with no long climbs. I run a nondescript 1:55:31 but win my age group, beating out a guy named Billy Bob in the last two miles. The winner runs 1:16 which isn't too shabby-back to back 38 minute 10k's at altitude. Afterward, I run an additional 20 kilometers to total 40 for the day, or 25 miles. Elapsed time: 5 hours.

I'm pleased with my effort but feeling lonely which is one of the minuses of living life as a bachelor runner. The tradeoff is that I can go anywhere and do anything without having to worry about making someone else unhappy.

On Sunday I get a late start after attending church in Leadville again. Deciding to climb Hope Pass, I drive south on Highway 24 then turn right on the gravel Clear Creek Road toward Winfield. Struggling up the Colorado Trail I discover that after a week at altitude my body is at its low point in terms of acclimatization. The trail is steep, but it shouldn't be this hard. A couple wearing Ultimate Sport Vests and accompanied by their dog passes me on their way down the mountain. Above the tree line I encounter the same wind tunnel effect I found on Loveland Pass. At the top I'm able to hunker down on the lee side of the pass and eat my honey and peanut butter sandwich without being blown off my feet. On the way down I find the same two people and their dog coming up to meet me. Hiking Hope Pass is one thing, but doing repeats of Hope Pass is something else so when we pass I speak up.

"Training for a trail race?" I inquire.

"Sure am," he replies.

"Hardrock?"

"Yup," he says. His name is Glen Turner of Highlands Ranch, Colorado. He's a first timer at Hardrock. He and his wife and dog are doing a Hope Pass over and back from Twin Lakes. After Glen continues on his way, it occurs to me that this double climb and descent at the midway point on the Leadville Trail 100 course that exhausts many ultrarunners is similar to the final fifteen miles of the Hardrock course from Maggie Gulch to the finish that comes after most participants have been on the course for over 30 hours. Something to think about.

Monday, June 28, I decide to go for more altitude training, so I drive east on I-70 past Dillon to the Bakerville Exit and Steven's Gulch Road, the rough gravel entry to the trailhead for Greys Peak and Torreys Peak, two mountains over 14,000 feet high (called "fourteeners"). It's a pretty day, sunny and warm. The trail is well maintained. As I hike up the gulch, the barren ramparts of McClellan Mountain rise to my left. As the trail begins to switchback, patches of snow appear. Ascending, I come upon a hiker who is sitting down, resting. His face is swollen and he isn't feeling well. Apparently he climbed another fourteener yesterday and is still dehydrated from that effort. I suggest that he descend, eat and drink, and try his luck another day.

Loveland Pass is only a few miles to the northwest, and the same westerly winds that tore at me a few days ago are harassing me again. I decide to climb Torrey first, the lesser of the two peaks by three feet, so I cut across the top of the snow-filled basin and hike up a ridge to the summit at 14,267 feet. It's taken me 2 ½ hours to get here from the trailhead, and I have walked steadily, experiencing no distress along the way. Reversing down the ridge, I re-cross the snowfield to the Greys Peak trail. This is the kind of high altitude tramping through snow that exhausted me during the 1997 Hardrock race. Today, although I stop a couple of times to catch my breath, I complete the double traverse in good shape and continue to the top of Greys at 14,270 feet. On both summits I record my achievement on a Colorado Mountain Club register contained in a plastic cylinder. On Greys Peak I'm joined by a young woman who makes several calls on her cell phone to tell her friends she's on top of a fourteener. We, in turn, welcome a mountain goat that nonchalantly walks to within 50 feet of us. He turns down our offer to place a call for him.

Descending, I'm full of confidence that my training is progressing so well. I also think about the fact that when Ricky Denesik set his record of climbing all of Colorado's fourteeners in 14 days and 16 minutes in August of 1997, he took less than 2 ½ hours to do both Greys and Torreys in blizzard conditions, then climbed four more fourteeners that same day. Elapsed time: 6 hours.

On Tuesday, June 29, I return to Hope Pass for a Full Monty over and back. After parking on the Winfield side I take me 1½ hours to reach the top. I'm feeling much more comfortable than on Sunday. Descending to the bottom on the Twin Lakes side, I decide to run a little farther, crossing some streams full of snow runoff in the process. Turning around to retrace my steps, I'm on a narrow log across a stream when my foot slips, I pitch forward and instinctively reach out with my left hand to catch my fall. My left hand and right foot both land in the water. At first I'm worried about my foot because it's the ankle I sprained last year on Bear Creek Trail. But something feels wrong with my hand. Looking at it I find that my little finger is now shaped like a "W". It must be broken. Turning it over I discover a deep gash across the finger joint exposing raw meat. I can see white bone inside the cut.

My first thought is to be grateful that it's only my finger that is injured and not my leg. With a broken leg I could sit here for a long time before someone came by to help me. I must return to my vehicle and get to the hospital as quickly as I can. My main concern is to keep the wound clean because I don't want the kind of infection that almost cost Carolyn Erdman her leg last year when she fell and cut herself during a race in Utah. Blood dripping, I begin the long hike up Hope Pass. Every time I cross a stream I hold my hand in the cold, rushing water to clean the wound, stop the bleeding, and prevent swelling.

Throughout this entire incident I feel no pain in my hand, just dull throbbing. I have plenty of food and fluids with me. The weather is beautiful. The one tricky problem on the ascent is kick stepping my way over a 30-foot snowdrift at the top of the pass where I don't want to lose my balance and have to reach out again with my injured hand. After three hours of hiking I reach my vehicle and head for Leadville.

At St. Vincent General Hospital I stroll in the emergency door and, after some confusion about filling out forms, two EMTs, Terri and John, take over and begin cleaning the wound. After some x-rays and a phone call, Doctor Perna arrives. He has completed the Leadville 100 mile bike race so we have a shared interest in endurance sports. After viewing the x-rays Doctor Perna tells me the finger is dislocated, not broken. That's a relief but the finger bone has to be re-located. Grasping my finger, Dr. Perna pulls and the bone snaps back into its socket with an audible click. I'm expecting to pass out, but there's no pain, just some discomfort. The idea of what's about to happen is worse than the actuality. The doctor deadens my finger with an injection, sews it up, wraps it with a splint to immobilize it, and sends me on my way with a prescription for antibiotics. Elapsed time of workout: 6 hours. Hospital elapsed time: 3 hours.

On Wednesday, June 30, my day begins with a phone call. It's my younger brother, Bruce. He says hello, tells me the call is not about our mother, then falls silent. I can tell he's struggling with his emotions. Finally my sister-in-law, Christi, takes the phone and tells me Bruce has a non-malignant brain tumor and will undergo surgery on Friday, two days hence.

This news is like a thunderbolt out of a blue sky. Bruce is 48. He and I ran our first marathon together in Minneapolis 15 years ago. He suffers from asthma, so he no longer runs marathons, but he stays in reasonably good shape by playing ice hockey. It was after a game a week ago that he had his first indication that something wasn't right. It consisted of an episode where he formulated words in his mind, but nothing came out of his mouth. After the same thing happened several times the next day at his law office, he scheduled a doctor's appointment. While talking to the doctor he had another episode, so an appointment was made with a specialist and surgery was quickly scheduled.

The tumor is about an inch long, has been growing for a year, and is dangerously close to an artery in Bruce's brain. Apparently, the surgeon is optimistic. The success rate for this type of surgery is 85 percent.

The past few days I've been thinking about Joel, and the connection is unsettling. I call my kids in Tampa and give them the news. My son is especially close to Bruce. Everyone in my family is frightened and prayerful. My mother calls to tell me she will phone on Friday with the results of the operation. Following the calls I return to Silverthorne and climb Ptarmigan Peak again. Elapsed time: 4 hours.

Thursday, July 1, is my 57th birthday. I celebrate by driving in the direction of Keystone and the little town of Montezuma to hike the Lenawee Trail. This takes me up to 12,800 feet on a ridge overlooking Arapahoe Basin ski resort. On the way up I encounter a dozen mountain goats and eight mountain sheep. With their delicate legs and handsome horns, the sheep are elegant animals compared with the goats which resemble refugees from a vaudeville act with their shaggy coats and baggy pant-legs. Small tufts of goat wool stick to the spiky points of willow shrubs lining the trail.

Upon descending the Lenawee Trail I still have half the day left, so I hike up the Chihuahua Gulch jeep road. After crossing a couple of rampaging streams and doing some willow whacking, I wind up scrambling up a steep rock glacier to a high basin at 12,400 feet that contains the still frozen Chihuahua Lake surrounded by rugged peaks. Most of the day my mind is occupied by thoughts of Bruce and how much he enjoys skiing in the Colorado mountains. Returning to the condo after eight hours of hiking in the wind and sun, I'm fatigued and troubled by what tomorrow might bring.

Friday, July 2, I climb Mt. Victoria (11,785 feet) located right on the edge of Frisco. The stiff climb reminds me of ascending Hope Pass. Elapsed time: 3 hours. I planned to drive down to Silverton today, but instead will wait for news about Bruce. Denver airport is only an hour and a half from Frisco. If the news is bad I can be in Minneapolis by this evening. I spend a few hours cleaning the condo, fix myself lunch, then wait. He is scheduled for surgery at 8 a.m. It should take 3-4 hours. Colorado is an hour earlier than Minnesota so I should receive a call around 1 p.m.

One p.m. comes and goes. I look at a magazine, check my watch, and wait, thinking that if no one is calling then the news must be bad. Three p.m., still nothing. Finally, at 4:30 I can't wait any longer and phone my mother. She sounds surprised by my call. I think that basically they had forgotten about me. The surgery took three hours and was successful. Bruce is resting in the intensive care unit and will go home on Tuesday. The tumor wasn't attached to anything. It was just sitting on top of his brain growing for a year like a pearl in a clam shell and finally made itself known by putting pressure on the speech center of his brain. After calling my kids to tell them Bruce will be fine I drive to Montrose where I spend the night.

Saturday, July 3, I drive to Silverton, check in at the Triangle Motel, and rendezvous with Helen and John Stergius, my Hardrock pacers. I know the Stergius's from Fayetteville. John is in the Army and last year when he was transferred from Fort Bragg to Fort Carson in Colorado Springs I asked him if he wanted to help me at Hardrock. Never having visited the San Juans, he jumped at the idea. Both John and Helen are experienced marathoners, and Helen has a couple of ultras under her belt. I want to show them the parts of the course where they will be with me, so we drive over to Maggies Gulch and climb Buffalo Boy Ridge. On top of the ridge with a great view of Green Mountain is a small granite monument, the final resting place of Bob Green, inscribed with some outdoor scenes and "Gone Fishing. Rest in Peace, 1940-1995."

After paying our respects to Bob we descend to Maggie Gulch road and drive over to Cunningham Gulch where we go up to Dives-Little Giant Pass and come down. Elapsed time: 7 hours. Helen and John enjoy the climbs. I'm confident they are prepared for next Saturday.

The area including the slopes of King Solomon Mountain, Little Giant Peak and Basin, Silver Lake, Arrastra Basin and Gulch-where we were hiking today and which are crossed by the final miles of the race-was the heart of early mining activity in Silverton. Silver Lake Mine, the Iowa and Royal Tiger mines, all perched on the edge of Silver Lake at 12,000 feet, produced gold and silver in the 1890's. Later, in the 1920's, the Shenandoah-Dives mine was developed in Arrastra Gulch. Single miners working at the Shenandoah Mine lived in a boarding house called the Spotted Pup.

That evening, lying in bed at the motel, I try to imagine what inspired people a hundred years ago when they were naming places in the San Juans-mines, mountains, rivers. Some were Indian names like "Ouray," the Ute chief who presided over treaty negotiations with the US government in the 1870's. Others, like *"Animas,"* were left over from the Spanish explorers. Many have mining connections. "Telluride" is the ore formed when the element tellurium combines with other metals. Some have European origins. For example, "Dives" means "rich man" in Welsh. *"Arrastra,"* a Spanish word, was a stone floor where gold-bearing ore was crushed by millstones dragged in circles by burros. Back in those days, imagination seems to have been in short supply. Three different Bear Creeks cross the Hardrock course. Couldn't they do any better than Red Mountain 1, 2 and 3? And who brain-stormed Cement Creek?

What bothers me most is the word *"gulch"*, an inelegant designation that appears repeatedly on maps of the San Juans. A gulch is supposed to be a deep narrow defile, especially one marking the course of a stream or torrent. The word is probably related to *gulch throat*, a drunkard. How undignified. I'm not suggesting that these places be renamed "gullies," which is just as bad as *gulch*. What I'd like to see is greater care taken in categorizing physical features characterized by steep slopes with flowing water at the bottom. Some qualify as ravines. Others are definitely canyons. A few might be gorges, a fine category with its connotations of unrelieved splendor. Certainly Cunningham, a thousand feet deep with nearly vertical sidewalls a quarter of a mile apart, should be a gorge. I drift off to sleep wondering, What's in a name?

Sunday, July 4, starts off at 7:30 a.m. with the Silverton Blue Ribbon 10K road race. There's nothing special about the course except that it is hilly and kicks my butt. I manage to get around the 6.2 miles in 1:02, an all time personal worst for the distance. After breakfast at the Lunch Box, Helen, John, lots of tourists, other runners, townies, and I watch the Silverton Fourth of July parade. This year the Colorado Department of Transportation snow removal trucks and road graders lead off followed by some Vietnam-era military vehicles, various old wrecks, unicyclists, jugglers, motorcyclists, horses and riders, the Silverton Brass Band, kids pulling wagons loaded with their brothers and sisters, the Silverton Gunfighters, the Silverton theater group, and anyone else who wants to dress up in an old-timey costume and walk down Greene Street waving at the spectators. Fire trucks bring up the rear. Each year the parade ends with a free-for-all water fight where volunteer fire fighters from Silverton and neighboring towns train their high pressure hoses on each other. Anyone who gets caught in the crossfire is knocked down by a water blast.

Looking up and down the street I can identify other Hardrock runners among the crowd. They are the lean ones with deep tans and calves like bowling balls, wearing Montrail shoes, shorts, 100-mile race t-shirts, sun glasses, and billed caps, with scrapes and cuts on their shins. Jon Stenious, former editor of the *Silverton Standard and the Miner* newspaper, liked to say that Hardrock runners are the ones who look like they're made out of leather and catmeat. Leslie Hunt and Kerry Trammell are here fresh from finishing Western States. I've seen Matt Mahoney riding around on his mountain bike. Eric Robinson drove in from Berkeley yesterday. Carolyn Erdman lives in Silverton. After pacing Joel in '97, Carolyn entered the race last year, but ran out of gas at the 80-mile point. That's better than I did.

After the parade, the Stergius' and I go over to Ouray where I show them the Bear Creek Trail. John will be pacing me there on Friday night, but it will be dark, so I want to show them what we won't be able to see during the race. On the trail we meet some people from Durango who ask us about the Hardrock race and are very supportive. All the strangers I have met on trails in the last two weeks have wished me well in the race. It's been a wonderful experience.

On Monday, July 5, I'm not quite sure what I want to do, but I wind up driving northeast out of Silverton on State Road 110, past Grouse Gulch, and park on the other side of Animas Forks. From there I hike on the gravel road past some mine ruins and 15 foot snowdrifts to the top of California Gulch, turn around and run down, then walk up to the top of Placer Gulch and run down, overtaking two slow moving Alpine Loop jeep tour vehicles along the way. Elapsed time: 4 hours, all above tree line and with the two high points at 13,000 feet.

After eating a BLT with hash browns at the Lunch Box, I drive over to Ouray, browse in the Buckskin Trading Bookstore, then decide to preview the course in and out of Ouray. Leaving my car in the Ouray Town Park, I walk/run over to where the course crosses the Uncompaghre River. Uncompaghre is a Ute word meaning "red lake." On the way back I discover John DeWalt, Gary Wright, Mike Dobies, and his friend, Sue Thompson, who are staying at a campground. John is living in his van that is a big mess crammed full of boxes containing smelly running shoes, clothes, and all kinds of packaged food. John is a 63 year old vegetarian. A few years ago he retired from his Pennsylvania health food store business. Now he winters in Florida where he doesn't run much but plays a lot of tennis. Every spring he gets in shape by running the Barkley Marathon, the Massanutten and Old Dominion 100 milers then comes out to Colorado and finishes the Hardrock race. Eight years ago John and I were of equal ability as far as ultrarunning goes but since then as I have slowed down he has gotten faster. I kid John about taking bee's pollen injections, but during the race he eats a lot of bread and butter. He explains his success by saying, "If you don't throw up during a race, then you aren't running as hard as you can."

Pondering this pearl of wisdom I decide it doesn't work for me. When I vomit during a race it means that I am dehydrated or that my stomach does not contain the right combination of fluids and electrolytes needed to digest the food I have been eating. My tipoff that I am pushing myself to my limit during a race is when I burst into tears.

Back in Silverton the smallness of my motel room is getting to me. I can barely turn around in the shower stall and when I sit on the toilet the wall is so close I have to bring my knees up to my chest. This setup reminds me of a basement apartment I rented when I was in graduate school. The basement wasn't divided into rooms. The stove was right next to the toilet so I could take a poop and fry an egg at the same time.

Every night in Silverton is a culinary adventure. Tonight I wander over to Blair Street looking for supper. Stepping into the Bent Elbow restaurant I find the place empty except for a single woman sitting at a table. I ask if I can join her and she turns out to be the owner of the restaurant, Melissa Gillon. The place is closed, but Melissa and I fall into an hour long conversation about our lives. Two lonely people. Melissa is an example of the strong, independent women that are attracted to Silverton. She's raising six kids alone while running her business. I wind up eating supper at the Brown Bear restaurant on Green Street then stop off at the TNT Grocery across from the motel for my nightly Eskimo Pie ice cream treat.

Tuesday, July 6. The question of when to start tapering for the race has arisen. I want to be well rested, but still feel sharp. Ideally, I should be sleeping at 12,000 feet to maximize my acclimatization, but I'm not much of a camper. I decide to begin backing off today and just hang around Silverton.

The town, like other Colorado mining towns, was laid out on a grid with little regard to esthetics. Lots are long and narrow-25 feet wide by 100 feet long-so the Victorian era houses are of similar dimensions. If you want to build a modern home in Silverton, you need to buy at least three lots. Only Greene Street is paved, so the old houses on Reese and Snowden streets, the upscale side of town, face gravel roads. Being surrounded by mountains means there are no bad views in Silverton, but the older houses don't have enough windows to take advantage of the wonderful scenery. I suspect that the miners who lived here at the turn of the century and labored in the mountains weren't interested in the views. Many of them died of exposure complicated by miner's consumption and pneumonia. Others froze to death when caught outside in a blizzard or an avalanche. Some committed suicide brought on by depression, alcoholism and drug addiction.

Two monuments have been erected to commemorate the town's mining heritage. The Christ of the Mines shrine on the lower slope of Anvil Mountain was built in 1958-59 when all of San Juan County's mines were closed and the area was in a horrible economic slump. Volunteers constructed the shrine alcove out of local stone from the Old Fischer Brewery. The 12-ton statue of Christ was carved in Italy from Carrara marble, the same stone Michelangelo used.

Two plaques are attached to the statue. On one is written, "This shrine erected in honor of Christ of the Mines by the people of Silverton to ask God's blessing on the mining industry of the San Juans, 1958-59."

The other plaque says, "In thanksgiving to Christ of the Mines for deliverance of entire work force when Lake Emma flooded Sunnyside Mine June 4 (Sunday, mine closed), 1978. St. Patrick Centennial, Aug. 15, 1982." St. Patrick's is the Catholic church in Silverton. Shortly after construction of the shrine was completed the Sunnyside Mine resumed operations.

People who stop at the shrine often leave wild flowers, small stones, and written messages in a wooden box next to the statue. One note says, "5-22-99. Dear God, Please help our good friend Pete. He was in a bad gun accident and is now fighting to survive. Thank you Lord. Guy and Esmeralda." Another says, "Dear God, Please help my son

Michael, let justice be served, help us to accept whatever is in store for us." On a third is written, "Dear God, Please help out daughter Lisa Ann with her drug and alcohol problem and to get on the right path, your path. Bill and Jolie."

The other monument is a new one, the *Parco del Emigrante*, located at the north end of Green Street. There, a marble stone is inscribed, "*Tirolesi Trentini*. San Juan Cty. In grateful recognition of the immigrants and their descendants from the province of Trento, Italy, who with strong will and desire to succeed with sacrifice of life, helped settle and develop Silverton, the San Juan Mountains and CO. *Tirolesi Trentini del Colorado*." Flanked by the US and Italian flags, the monument is topped by two angels in prayer and a small statue of a miner wielding a hand drill and hammer.

Across the street from the *Parco del Emigrante* is Silverton's Memorial Park, with its gazebo, toilets, picnic tables, horseshoe pitching area, and tennis and volleyball courts. A marble monument erected by American Legion Post 14 in 1998 is inscribed, "San Juan Cty CO. Dedicated in memory of Past, Present and Future Veterans" and includes the insignias of the five military services.

Next to the park are the San Juan County Archives building, the county courthouse, and the museum which is located in the old jail. Just a block to the south is the Town Hall across Green Street from the restored Wyman Hotel. All the official town and county buildings were erected in the early 1900's when the town was rolling in tax revenue.

Over on Reese Street, on the same block as the school, sits the Carnegie Library, erected in 1906. Town librarian, Jackie Leithauser, is married to the county sheriff. In past years Joel Zucker used the library's computer to keep up with his e-mail. I asked her what her impression was of Joel and she replied, "He was a wonderful man. All the kids in town called him Rumpelstiltskin."

Tuesday afternoon I drive down to Durango. On the way I spot a hand-lettered sign announcing "Gourmet Elk Jerky Just Ahead." Pulling off the highway I stop in front of a table loaded with plastic bags containing the dried meat and presided over by a hairy-looking mountain man. Rolling down my window I inquire, "What's the difference between regular elk jerky and the gourmet variety?"

The guy sports a bushy beard and is wearing a broad-brimmed western hat and bib overalls. "You don't understand," he informs me. "Elk jerky is by definition a gourmet food."

"Whose definition?" I reply.

"What do you mean, whose definition? It's not in the Bible. It's common knowledge."

"But don't all jerkies taste pretty much the same?" I ask. "I've eaten ostrich jerky and I couldn't tell the difference between it and beef jerky." He's not enjoying the interrogation. I continue bothering him. "So what's with the sign?" I ask.

"It's a marketing device."

"Marketing device? What are you, a Harvard MBA?" I'm getting warmed up.

"You stopped, didn't you?" Good point, but I'm not giving him the satisfaction of admitting it.

"Can I have a free sample?"

"No."

"Then how am I supposed to decide if it's gourmet or regular?"

"This is where we started, isn't it? Excuse me. You'll have to move your vehicle. My customers can't pull in here if you are parked in front of my table."

I feel like turning this fellow in to the La Plata County Better Business Bureau for false advertising, but don't really have the time to pursue it today.

Once in Durango I get a haircut, buy some fruit and some shoe inserts, and stop by the railroad station to talk to Russell Steel. Born in West Virginia, Russell is a street artist who came out to Durango years ago. He paints watercolor scenes of the San Juans and the Durango and Silverton Narrow Gauge Railroad and sells them to tourists. He peddles between his house and the station on a contraption of a bicycle that he has modified to carry his easel and other equipment. Today the temperature is in the 90's and he's complaining that the heat is thickening his paint and making it hard to work.

Back in Silverton this evening I telephone my brother who is home from the hospital. He tells me that lying on the operating table his thoughts were with his family. "Life is precious," Bruce says; "value every minute of it."

On Wednesday eighty people gather in the Silverton school gym for Joel Zucker's memorial service. During the winter, boys and girls high school and JV basketball games in the old building are a focal point of community activity. Climbing ropes dangle from the ceiling, and basketball goals hang at both ends. Wooden bleachers occupy the side walls and a stage stands at one end. A climbing wall has been erected in one corner, and the school symbols (a crossed pick and shovel) are painted on the walls. Chairs have been set up on the basketball floor.

Andi Kron has organized the service to celebrate Joel's life and commemorate *Yahrzeit*, the one year anniversary of his death. Lynne Zucker, Joel's mother, is there, as is his aunt, Robin Steinberg. Although Joel was raised as a Jew, he stopped being observant after his *bar mitzvah* when he was 13. Everyone recites the Mourners Kaddish which asks God to bring comfort to the bereaved and grant the departed grace and mercy. Then those who want to speak come forward. Many bring laughs, a few produce tears.

Charlie Thorn recalls Joel's regard for a book called *Man's Search for Meaning* by Victor Frankel. It's the story of Frankel's survival of a Nazi concentration camp where everything was taken from him except his self respect. Brian Scott speaks about finding something missing in Silverton this week-Joel's winning smile. Carolyn Erdman talks about Joel's love of Hardrock and how he touched people. Ulli Kamm remembers Joel's enjoyment of the entire 48 hours of the race and his absolute joy upon finishing. Ginny La Forme talks about Joel's friendliness and how he made her feel as if she were part of the race. Steve Pattillo recalls Joel's tidiness and how interested he was in the small details of race preparation. Blake Wood talks about his lengthy e-mail correspondence with Joel and how everyone who knew him felt close to him. Dale Garland describes Joel's method of using the dogs he was exercising as an excuse to meet women on the streets of Silverton. Chuck Haraway demonstrates Joel's dog greeting technique by kneeling down on all fours and exchanging licks with his own dog, Annie. Jim Fischer remarks that Joel taught him not to hold anything back and remembers Joel telling aid station volunteers, "You've got to treat me special; I'm the shortest person in the race."

Andi and Charlie have established the Joel Zucker Memorial Fund Scholarship, a $500.00 award presented to the graduating senior from Silverton High School who is outstanding in athletics and will be attending college. Lars Gibson, who excelled at track, cross country, and basketball, and is interested in mechanical engineering, is the first recipient of the award. Both Lars and his mother speak. Although they did not know Joel and seem a little bewildered by the occasion, they are grateful for the scholarship.

After the service, a dozen people drive over to Mineral Creek campground with the idea of hiking up to the top of Grant Swamp Pass were Joel's plaque has been placed. It rained last night, so the creeks are high. At the first stream crossing, Joel's mother decides she has had enough and turns back. I'm not keen on trashing my legs two days before the race, so I bail out where the Hardrock course intersects the Ice Lake Trail. A couple of people, Matt Mahoney and Jim Fischer, go all the way to the pass at 13,000 feet. Walking back to the parking lot I catch up with Lynne Zucker. She talks mainly about Joel's dad, Arnie, whom Joel disliked intensely, but apparently resembled. I suspect the old man made life miserable for the scrawny kid who stuttered.

Charlie Thorn carboloading during the race. Photo by Andi Kron

On Wednesday afternoon Charlie presents the long briefing complete with slides at the Miners Union Theater on 11th street just off Greene Street upstairs above the Miners Tavern. Walt and Judy Esser arrived in Silverton today, and

Walt joins me for the briefing. Charlie is famous for his thoroughness and takes two hours to go over every inch of the route. He says of the course, "We tried to put it as far away from civilization as possible." I follow along with Charlie in the course notes of my Hardrock Runners Manual, littering the margins with comments like "Stay Strong Here" and "Don't Lose Heart Here." Typically, before a race I'm full of pipe dreams about running fast and having the race of my life. Going over the trail in such detail brings a flood of recognition of just how difficult it is. I remember that I already had the race of my life at the Vermont 100 in 1991 and leave the theater depressed about my chances of ever finishing Hardrock.

That evening Judy, Walt, and I eat fried chicken at the Chattanooga Café. Two weeks ago Walt finished Western States, but thoroughly trashed his quads. He's still limping on badly blistered feet and won't be able to pace me on the final eight miles from Cunningham aid station to the finish. If John survives the first night with me, I'll ask him to take Walt's place.

On Thursday morning I wake up early, wash my clothes at the laundromat across the street from the motel, and meet Judy and Walt for breakfast of pancakes, hash brown potatoes, and whole wheat toast at the Lunch Box. We take our time eating then walk over to the school gym to check in for the race. At the check-in table, I sign my Colorado Hiking Certificate. My race number this year is 104. The race shirt is blue capilene with the course profile on the back, a departure from previous years when we were given white Henley style collarless shirts with a scene from the Hardrock course screened on the back. For some reason a new "HRH" logo has replaced the old "wild and tough" ram's head logo on the shirt front. This is a step in the wrong direction. Why screw around with a winning design?

Feeling a little grumpy, I go over to the medical table. Dr. Kathy Lang takes my pulse, 72, and measures my blood pressure, 138/68, and writes the information on a hospital ID band that she attaches to my wrist. I ask her to look at my finger. It's time to take out the stitches. She tells me to wash my hand then she re-bandages my finger with a new type of elastic wrap. After that I hang out for a while waiting for the pre-race briefing and visiting with my buddies Rollin Perry and Jim Benike, who were both at the Ice Age 50. Jim hurt his shin at the Ice Age race two months ago and claims he hasn't run since. He finished Hardrock in 1997, so he's hoping his experience will carry him through a second time. I'm not so sure.

Ordinarily everyone sits in the bleachers for the briefing but so many people are here they have put chairs on the gym floor to accommodate everybody. Gordon Hardman, the Rhodesia-born engineer who lives in Boulder, Colorado, and the man who had the original idea for the race, welcomes the runners, their families, and crews. Previously, Gordon always made a weak joke during his remarks, "We have a proud tradition here. Nobody's ever died at this race." This year he mumbles his regrets about Joel then quickly points out that lots of flowers are blooming on the course and that he saw two snakes while he was training. Snakes aren't supposed to be able to survive at this altitude, but apparently it's a subtle sign of global warming. Personally, I think Gordon was hallucinating when he spotted the snakes.

Dale Garland, the race director, is next. A school teacher in Durango, Dale is acting alone this year since his former co-race director, Kristina Maxfield, resigned after last year's event. Dale introduces Chris Nute, Silverton Town Board member and the only local ever to finish the race.   C h r i s isn't running this year because his wife is expecting a baby any day now. Chris wishes us good luck then San Juan County Sheriff Greg Leithauser tells us the county search and rescue team is prepared to help in case anyone gets lost. Rick Ryan, the Bureau of Land Management (BLM) representative informs the crowd that the race takes us through two BLM resource areas, five ranger districts, and four national forests.

At about this point I notice that it's raining outside. Not a good sign.

Dale introduces Dino Darling, who has replaced Jim Scott as the new communications director, and Lisa Richardson, a BLM employee who coordinates the aid stations. Commenting that "the mind can process only what the rear end can handle," Dale promises that Charlie's short trail briefing will only last an hour. The only major change in the course is the different start/finish location, that is in front of the gym this year. There's more snow than last year, but not as much as in '97. My mind wanders. I'm beginning to fold inward, to withdraw inside myself in order to conserve energy and narrow my focus prior to the start of the race. I picture myself as an arrow, stripped to the essentials. I'm cutting out distractions, paying less attention to my surroundings, almost becoming autistic in my self-centeredness. It's something that happens naturally to me before 100 mile races, a sort of unconscious meditation on survival, concentrating my inner resources on the task at hand. I respond to questions but all I'm thinking about now is the physical, emotional, and mental demands that will be made on me during the next two days. I feel like a *gyoja* preparing himself for an ordeal.

Charlie completes his briefing and Dale contributes his Reader's Digest version of the brief, "If there's a hill, run up it; if there's a river, run through it." He then introduces Gordon Hardman, Kirk Apt, and Ulli Kamm, the five-time Hardrock finishers in attendance, and warns that course cutters will be disqualified. More runners than ever before, 117, are signed up. Dale's final advice, parodying Ken Chlouber, is, "If you drop out you disappoint your country, your mother, and your dog." As the meeting is breaking up, I hear John DeWalt yell, "Is there drug testing?" This is an in-joke carrying on a Joe Clapper, Virginia Happy Trails Running Club tradition.

As far as I'm concerned, after five 50-mile races, one marathon, three 50-kilometer races, an adventure race that took 26 hours to complete, three rugged eight hour Blue

Ridge training runs, two months of 80-90 mile training weeks, speed work, hill work, and mental gymnastics-all in the last nine months-topped off with three weeks of living at 9000 feet of altitude, climbing two 14,000 foot peaks, running and hiking six to eight hours every day in the mountains, I'm as ready as I'll ever be.

Book 3

The Race

"To finish one must only not quit."
                    Milan Milanovich, 1997

Thursday night before the race is filled with the usual nervousness. An owl calling in the darkness wakes me. I get out of bed to pee six times, checking the clock on each occasion. Finally 4:30 a.m., Friday, July 9, arrives. I've been waiting for this moment for six months. Turning on the bed light I reach for my glasses. I purchased a new container of Bag Balm in Frisco and proceed to dab the anti-chaffing ointment under my arms, on my nipples, my crotch and my feet. Carefully, I attach the splint to my injured left little finger. Pulling on my new green Rail Rider shorts with the deep front pockets, I put on a long sleeve white shirt with side vents and tie a red bandana around my neck. A pair of light weight polypropolene gloves go into one of the pockets of my shorts, and I pin my number on the front of my shorts. Last are a brand new pair of Thorlo socks, my size 12 Nike Armas, and a pair of Jim O'Brian gaiters to keep the sticks and stones out of my shoes.

While I'm dressing I manage to choke down a peach, my vitamin pills, some orange juice, a blueberry yogurt, a can of Equate Plus (the less expensive Wal-Mart version of Ensure Plus), and half a chocolate muffin. I'll be wearing my Ultimate Sport Vest instead of a butt pack, so I fill the 80-oz fluid container with Succeed Amino energy drink, and fill the front vest pockets with Powerbites; Powergels; GU; a sandwich bag filled with Succeed sodium and potassium tablets; another sandwich bag containing toilet paper together with some matches, a plastic spoon; two Compeed blister patches; a space blanket; a copy of the written course description which I reduced by 50% on my office photocopying machine; my Colorado Hiking Certificate; and my prescription sunglasses in their case. I'm carrying a 30-oz plastic bottle filled with half water and half Mountain Dew. I tie a small bag containing a nylon windbreaker onto the vest. Hanging an emergency whistle on a string around my neck, I don my lucky yellow Powerbar hat and I'm out the motel room door by 5:30.

Walking across Greene Street to the Prospector Motel, I find the Essers waiting for me in the parking lot. We walk over to the school gym where the Stergius's are waiting for us. They arrived in town at 3 a.m. and slept in their vehicle parked on Reese Street outside the gym. Filled with apprehension, I enter the gym, check in, and look around. Rick Trujillo is standing next to me looking stricken.

I ask him, "Are you acclimated and in good shape?"

He responds, "I'm worried about a torn muscle in my calf."

Race director Dale Garland calls out, "Five minutes to go."

Judy Esser takes some photographs of me and the Stergius's. I point out Ricky Denesik, telling her. "He's all legs and lungs."

We begin moving out into 12th Street where the Hardrock rock we're supposed to kiss when we finish the race has been relocated from its usual spot in the Kendall Mountain

Recreation Area parking lot. Skies are brightening as we mill around in the street. I drop to one knee for my usual pre-race prayer, "God give me the strength to complete this race and save me from injury." Among the runners is Mike Luther of Silverton, the only genuine Hardrock miner ever to enter the race.

Joe Riddle, my running buddy from Lenoir, North Carolina, is standing next to me. Garland is counting down the last ten seconds before the start. When he yells GO my watch shows 22 seconds past 6 a.m.

Jogging a short distance up 12th Street we turn left on Snowden Street. I'm breathing noisily through my nose and mouth waiting for my heart rate to catch up with my leg speed. As we commence our adventure, Lance Armstrong is leading the Tour de France. Our Hardrock peloton turns right on 10th Street, and everyone slows to walk uphill to the Shrine Road. On Shrine Road I notice that Rick Trujillo is in the lead, but that's the last I will see of any frontrunners.

Running southwest down the Shrine Road, we turn right on a jeep road just before Highway 550 onto the Nute Chute, the new trail added to the course last year to replace a short highway section. At last year's long briefing John Cappis gloated, "No more free ride to the finish on Highway 550," when he announced the course change. He even put an orienteering punch on a piece of plywood next to the trail which runners had to use on their numbers to show they had not taken the road. I thought that was a little overzealous. The trail was suggested by Chris Nute.

I call out, "We're on the Nute Chute." Ernst Baer of Durango is just ahead of me and shouts back, "Isn't that Shoot Nute?"

By this time my breathing has regularized. Joe Riddle is still next to me. He says, "I was glad you were breathing hard at the start so I wasn't the only one."

"It takes a little time for my cardio-vascular system to spin up. I'm all right now," I reply.

Joe has been in Silverton for a week. At the Holiday Lake 50K race in March, both David Horton and I advised Joe that it was a waste of time and money to attempt Hardrock without three weeks of training at altitude, but like most ultrarunners, Joe is hardheaded and decided to enter even though he could only afford to invest a single week to prepare for the race. Joe's been balancing a job, family life, and running ultras for a long time, so today I manage to keep my mouth shut and not remind him of the three week rule. It's too late anyway. The race is on. This trail used to be the bed for the Silverton Railroad which ran roughly parallel to the current Highway 550 from Silverton north to the mining area around Ironton, now a ghost town on the Ouray side of Red Mountain Pass.

After 2 1/2 miles of running through an aspen forest, we angle left downhill, cross the highway, and lumber past a crowd of cheering crew members and townspeople to get in line to cross Mineral Creek just above its confluence with Silverton Bear Creek (so called to distinguish it from the two other Bear Creeks on the course). This will probably be the last time for the next 48 hours that my feet will be dry. Feeling like a circus performer, I step into the icy water and grip the rope that has been strung across Mineral Creek. The technique here is to face upstream while side stepping through the knee deep water and praying that I don't get knocked off my feet by the current. That would produce a roar from the onlookers.

Once safely out of the water and ascending the old mining trail into Bear Creek canyon, I comment to Joe, "Compared with the rest of the course this first long climb is a treat."

Joe replies, "I'm just glad to be out here enjoying the mountains and learning about this race." Joe knows all about my history of failures at Hardrock, so he isn't making any predictions about his own result. As usual, he is faster than I am early in the race so he moves ahead in the forest as runners pass each other in their efforts to find a comfortable pace. It's twelve miles from the start to the first aid station, the longest part of the course without aid.

With Bear Mountain on my right and Sultan Mountain on my left I move across rock slides and through willow bushes. Finding myself behind Ulli Kamm we break out of the woods and climb above tree line. Stopping briefly to turn around and admire the view of Sultan Mountain, Ulli comments, "It's great to be alive."

"Beats the heck out of the alternative," I respond.

Departing the Bear Creek drainage area we join the Putnam Basin trail, climb into Putnam Basin itself, and eventually reach the Putnam-Lime Creek saddle. Carrying on to our right up a ridge, we top out at 12,600 feet, the end of the first major climb, eight miles from the start.

From this point the course makes a sharp left turn, and we plunge down a steep hillside in the first of many straight line descents. Charlie Thorn is a man with an affinity for direct approaches, and this is his course. Throughout the two days of the race, many runners will be muttering unkind things about Charlie's concept of a challenging course. As he says, "Hardrock exists inside my head a lot more than it exists in the San Juan Mountains. In fact, Hardrock doesn't even exist in the San Juans unless I'm up there, by force of will, bringing it into existence."

The descent bottoms out in a meadow which we cross between the upper Cataract Gulch on our right and the Cataract-Lime Creek saddle on our left. By now the Hardrock peleton has separated as runners of equal abilities find each other and form small groups. In each of my attempts at Hardrock I have found myself running with the same individuals, at least until I fell behind and dropped out. These include Ulli, the German-born five-time finisher, who found a job in Colorado and immigrated to the US after he fell in love with the Hardrock. Although they are behind us at this point, Roger Wiegand, Carl Yates, and Rollin Perry will catch up with us later. We're the over the hill gang. I'm 57. Roger, 56, is a three-time Hardrock non-finisher. At 72, Carl is the oldest entrant in the race. He finished Hardrock in 1993 when he was 65. Rollin, 60, is a three-time finisher. Only 49, Jim Ballard, a college math teacher from Montana and two-time Hardrock finisher, is also part of the group. Each July we find ourselves joined together in our dedication to enduring and in our striving to achieve the same goal-to finish the Hardrock 100.

A mine trail takes us west through or around several snowfields and splashing through some slippery willow bogs. The mush underfoot soaks quickly through my socks and shoes. Huge amounts of water pour out of the San Juans from natural springs and melting snow. Descending on a sheep herder's trail into the Porcupine Creek drainage, I keep watching for the log at the edge of the trail where we turn left. At the long briefing there was derisive snorting and laughter from first-timers when Charlie mentioned specific logs or tree stumps at crucial turns on the course. Apparently, these people couldn't believe that out of 100 miles of wild and tough terrain they were supposed to identify particular trees here and there, but concentration on the details of the course description can mean the difference between success and failure in this race, more than any other 100 miler. Race veterans nodded sagely at Charlie's mention of these course markers. The log appears and the turn is well marked with flags and ribbons. The trail takes me below the tree line and across repeated tributaries of Porcupine Creek.

Descending westward from over 11,000 feet through spruce and pine trees I traverse the northeast slope of the Twin Sisters, both thirteeners, and cross under an active rock glacier. As Charlie puts it in the written course description, "The grass on the hillside is visibly being displaced by the moving rock....one of nature's mountain eroding activities in action."

Concentrating on my footing, I don't have time to ponder the ageless process of mountain erosion as I descend a series of switchbacks. At the bottom of the hill there is a fork in the path. From two years ago I remember to take the right fork, work my way on swampy ground through some willows, and arrive at the South Fork of Mineral Creek, the twelve-mile point. Thirty feet of wading through knee-deep water isn't bad. I recall being knocked off my feet here by the current during a training run in 1997. I wonder how fast I could go if somehow I could transfer the energy of the rushing water to the bones and muscles of my legs the way water energy is transformed into electricity, or wind energy is caught by a sail to power a boat. In a way I guess this happens when I soak my tired legs in cold water to take the stiffness out of them after a long run.

The grassy hillside on the other side of the South Fork is full of blooming wild flowers following recent rains, blue columbines and marsh marigolds. Two four-wheel drive vehicles are parked at the top of the hill on Bandora Road, their occupants watching us hike up to the road. Ulli speaks to them as he passes by, but I remain silent. Reaching the road I turn right and jog a quarter of a mile down to the Kamm Traverse (KT) aid station, elevation 10,640 feet, at the 12.2-mile point. I call out, "104, checking in." It's 10 a.m. I'm right on time.

At the aid station I ask to have my water bottle filled with half Coke and half water. I recognize a volunteer from last year who impressed me with his extensive tattooing, face piercing, and especially his ear lob plugs.

"Hey, weren't you at Maggie Gulch last year?" I yell.

Smiling at the recollection, he replies, "Yes, they like to move us around." The ear lob plugs remind me of Indians in the Amazon River basin and old Zulu women in South Africa. After drinking several cups of water, eating a cookie, and grabbing a banana, I'm out of the aid station.

"104, checking out."

"Good luck," chorus the volunteers.

"Thanks, I'll need it." Next aid station: 6.6 miles.

I'm on the Kamm Traverse, a trail not quite one mile long that follows the slope contour. This section of the course is named for Ulli, who suggested it in 1993 after studying some old maps of the area. KT replaced a far easier route used in the first two iterations of the race and probably added two hours to the time required to finish the race. Some runners complained that the race organizers were making the course too difficult for ordinary runners like myself to complete in under 48 hours. Charlie Thorn's response to the criticism was, "I have a confession. It ain't easy."

Curiously, the southeast facing slope I'm on is covered with wild flowers, especially purple columbines, but totally denuded of trees, while across the valley to my right the sides of Porcupine Creek are occupied by an army of fir trees. Maybe this entire slope is one big mine dump where trees won't grow. One thousand feet below me lies the South Mineral Campground with its RVs, tents, and four-wheel drive vehicles seemingly in miniature. The course description warns of Exposure and Acrophobia here, but the view is too stunning for either to bother me.

At the front of the race a group of a dozen men came through the KT aid station at 8:53 a.m., already over an hour ahead of me. Among them were Ricky Denesik and Andrew Lapkass. Two years ago Lapkass had a "shot from guns" start, came through KT at 8:35, a half hour ahead of everyone else, and dropped out at Ouray. This year he warmed up for the race by climbing Mount Everest. Rick Trujillo's injured calf muscle has taken him out of the race and he never checks into KT. The first three women, Betsy Kalmeyer, of Steamboat Springs, Colorado, Sue Johnston, who lives in Waterford, Vermont, and Betsy Nye, 35, of Tahoe City, California, came through together at 9:08 a.m.

Although Steamboat Springs is at 7000 feet, Betsy Kalmeyer arrived in Silverton a week ahead of time to acclimatize and learn the course. After snow shoeing and skiing all winter, she has been building up her weekend long runs to ten hours. Her goal is to improve her '96 time and finish Hardrock in 35 hours. In Tahoe City, Betsy Nye is surrounded by superb mountain trails. Squaw Valley, where the Western States 100 miler begins, is only a 15-minute drive from where Betsy lives. Betsy trains occasionally with Laura Vaughan, the current Hardrock women's record holder. Living at altitude, the two Betsys have an advantage over Sue, but she flew out to Albuquerque on June 20 and arrived in Silverton on the 25th, so she has had time to acclimate. She is an experienced mountaineer, rock climber, and trail runner who through-hiked the Appalachian Trail in 1994 and is the women's record holder at the Massanutten 100. Hardrock should be her kind of course.

Half way across the traverse at a caved-in mine portal, the abandoned road I have been following turns into a faint game trail. The phrases, "faint game trail" and "faint animal trail," used by Charlie in his course briefings, have never failed to produce laughter from his audience, acknowledging them as a code for some beaten down grass, but nothing that resembles a real trail. In this case, however, the Hardrock runners have been using this route for five years and a true trail is beginning to emerge.

Entering the trees, I follow the flags through some wet areas. Suddenly, I slip on the wet grass, my feet fly up, and I land heavily on my back. My Sport Vest absorbs some of the blow, but I have reached back with both hands to catch myself and have crunched my injured little finger. It hurts and the thought flashes through my mind that I have injured it again. A second thought assures me that I run on my feet, not on my hands, and I can still finish the race. Clutching my finger I sit there until the pain ebbs.

The Hardrock 100 course offers several varieties of falls. One is the "slippery" fall, usually on mud or wet grass, like the one that I just took where you land on your backside. Another is the "too steep" fall, where it's impossible to remain upright while going downhill. Usually, this results in a baseball slide where one leg is tucked underneath while the other sticks straight out. I'm always surprised when I survive a "too steep" fall with no broken bones. A third type is the "hidden stump" or its variant, the "hidden rock" fall-the most spectacular of the falls in that usually all four limbs fly out in different directions and the landing is a one pointer on the face or chest. Standing up, I dust myself off and continue down to the Lower Ice Lake Basin Creek. With a waterfall on my left, the creek here is raging, full of snowmelt from the basin above.

Carolyn Erdman near the top of Grant–Swamp pass. Photo by David Emory/HRH

Yesterday on our aborted hike to Joel's plaque, a group of us came through here and built a log bridge across the creek. Our bridge is gone today, but a couple of logs are lying at odd angles across the creek. Full of apprehension and recalling my misadventure on the Hope Pass trail, I venture out on them. They are slippery, but wedged firmly between some rocks, so I'm able to make my way safely to the other side. Here a stiff climb of several hundred yards faces me. Grabbing hold of several small trees to help propel myself up the hill, I emerge on the Ice Lake Trail, a popular route to the Ice Lake Basin. Recalling this from two years ago as a place where I must watch carefully for a right turn off the trail, I concentrate my attention, but when I reach the crucial place the change of direction is well marked with flags and ribbons, and I am relieved. This is a grassy area full of skunk cabbage. Skunk cabbage has a distinctive look about it but no offensive smell. Maybe it throws off a bad odor if it is cooked or its leaves are torn. I'm not pausing to investigate. Relentless forward motion is my mantra.

An old version of the Island Lake Trail, well flagged, urges me on the ascent, across a mine dump with pieces of iron track strewn about. As I top a ridge, Island Lake, a small tarn, appears on my left; US Grant Peak (13,767 ft.) lies ahead of me and my destination, Grant-Swamp Pass, comes into focus on my right. A string of half a dozen runners is stretched out ahead of me like human course markers so I can see the tack everyone is taking. Large scree fields offer precarious footing on both sides of the pass. On this, the southwest side of Grant-Swamp, runners have worn a trail that angles upward across the scree. The angle becomes acute at a certain point and a quick-footed scramble straight up the loose rock brings me to the top of the pass, climb number two in the race, at 12,920 feet.

This is a primitive place. I can't imagine what it must be like when the winter winds howl over this pass. The view of Swamp Canyon in front of me is breathtaking. This was Joel's favorite place on the course. Last year I had a problem with acrophobia up here during a training run and had to sit down in order to calm my distress. This year I'm not bothered. Joel's plaque is affixed to a large boulder on top of the pass. Picking up a stone, I add it to the pile under the plaque then I slap the plaque twice with my hand.

The plaque was designed and written by Andi Kron and Gail Wood. On it are a runner, two dogs, a mountain range silhouette, and these words: "Joel Zucker, October 6, 1953 * July 14, 1998. An inspired ultrarunner who loved dogs, the mountains and trails. A beloved companion, son and friend. He always had a word, a joke and a dog biscuit for everyone. Arf, Arf! Joel died shortly after completing his third Hardrock Hundred race. For him it was the ultimate challenge and his greatest achievement. May he run in peace. 'Whatever you think you can do or believe you can do, begin it. Action has magic, grace and power in it.' Goethe."

"Hope you're doin okay, Joel buddy." I visualize Joel grinning at me enjoying the runners passing by his vantage point. I wonder if birds visit his plaque. Native Americans believe that when there has been a sudden or untimely death, the spirit of the deceased is restless and rides the wind or flies with an eagle until it is ready to rest.

Joe Riddle has reached the top just ahead of me. Two years ago the descent into the canyon was a huge snow field which I glissaded tearing the backside out of my tights, bloodying my bottom, and tearing skin off my hands when I tried to slow my fall by using them as brakes in the icy snow. This year the snowfield is smaller and further to our right. Joe isn't sure which route to take.

"What do you think, Bob? The guy in front of us went around Joel's boulder and is taking the snow field."

I don't like the looks of maneuvering around Joel's boulder. Taking out my polypro gloves I pull one over my right hand in preparation for the descent. The bandage on my little finger prevents me from getting the other glove on my left hand. I'll just have to keep it out of harms way.

"This scree slope right in front of us seems like the surest way to the bottom," I reply.

Joe doesn't waste time discussing the pros and cons of my suggestion, but dives right off the top of the pass and starts sliding down the scree. When he is twenty yards down the steep slope, I follow. I try to walk down the rocks as they move along with me, like wading down an escalator, but the pass is too steep and I wind up sliding down with my right gloved hand acting as a brake on the rocks while holding my left hand up in the air, like I'm riding a bucking bronco. Occasionally, I kick up a rock that goes plummeting down in Joe's direction. This is where David Horton was injured last year when runners were going in the opposite direction climbing up this slope. Horton's pacer was climbing ahead of him and kicked up a rock that hurtled down smashing into David's hand. He was lucky the rock didn't hit him in the face. As it was he had a compound fracture, his finger bone protruding from the skin at an odd angle. David's competitive nature, his overpowering desire to run down Ricky Denesik and win Hardrock '98, kept him in the race when ordinary runners would have dropped out.

Another runner has jumped onto the scree above me and is descending. I call to him:

"Let us get further downhill before you follow so you don't kick rocks on us."

"All right, go ahead," he yells back just as a rock I dislodge goes tumbling in Joe's direction.

"Heads up for the rock, Joe." It nearly hits him. I want to get off this mountainside. This is why serious rock climbers wear protective helmets. People get killed in situations like this.

It's roughly 500 yards to the bottom. Once we get there Joe and I continue down Swamp Canyon on an ankle-breaking rock glacier. I notice Ulli is on my right, making good time running down a snowfield. As usual, Ulli's tactics are superior to mine, so I veer off and join him for a glissade down the snow leaving Joe behind to struggle through the rocks.

The course takes us left to a grassy bench that we follow around the head of Swamp Canyon and under the north face of US Grant peak. It's unusual to see anyone who isn't a runner at this location, but here we encounter two groups of people. One is a bunch of hikers, while members of the other group are course monitors writing down our numbers. Charlie didn't mention this in his briefing. Two years ago there was a punch here that we used to mark our numbers. This is his way of making sure that no one is deviating from the course. Apparently, one year instead of following the course markings, one runner took a faster route by continuing down Swamp Canyon and following the Ophir Pass Road into Chapman aid station. I'm petrified of losing the course markings, so I'm not about to attempt some short cut.

Crossing another rock field we finally enter a spruce/fir forest and find a trail that takes us downhill. Here I catch up with Jose Wilkie of Louisville, Kentucky. Like Jim Musselman, Jose plans to finish a dozen hundred-mile races this summer. He has already waltzed through Umstead, Old Dominion, and Massanutten, but I can tell by the pained look on his face that he isn't enjoying the Hardrock dance.

"Hey, Jose, how's it goin?" I enquire.

"Hey man, not so good," responds the Venezuelan born runner.

Actually, I'm a little alarmed by how bad he looks.

"You need some energy. How 'bout a Powergel?"

"No thanks, I've got some of that stuff."

Looks like I can't help.

"All right then, see you later." At Hardrock most runners discover in the first twenty miles how well prepared they are for the race.

Easy downhill trail running sends me into a reverie about Africa where I lived for ten years, first as a Peace Corps Volunteer high school teacher and later as a university lecturer. The names my students adopted were often good for a laugh. I usually had an Elvis sitting in my class plus a Wellington, and, once, Fidel Castro sat in the front row although he changed his name to Stalin half way through the year. My current favorite African name belongs not to one of my long-ago students but to a South African ultrarunner named Jetman Msuthu. Jetman-now there's a name for a runner. I try it on. Maybe it will make me rocket fast. "Jetman Boeder, King of the San Juans, today won the eighth annual Hardrock 100 Mile race setting a new course record."

Arriving at a gravel road snaps me out of my daydream. Which way do I go? Looking around for the flags I spot one to my left. This is Swamp Canyon Road where Jetman catches up with Margaret and Mark Heaphy of Missoula, Montana. I'm feeling a little strange but not goofy enough to introduce myself by my new running handle.

"Hey, you're the Heaphys. I'm Bob. What's going on? You're usually miles ahead of me at this point." Mark finished fourth overall in 1994 and fifth in 1997. Before she married, Margaret's last name was Smith. Margaret Smith won the women's title in the 1993 and 1994 races, but today she's using ski poles and is wearing braces on both knees.

Mark replies, "We decided to make Hardrock a family event this year."

I'm making better time than they are, tripping the light fandango down this rocky road.

"All right, see you at the aid station."

Joe has caught up to me. We're in an aspen grove now as we cross the San Miguel River on a log bridge, ford Ophir Creek coming out of Chapman Gulch, and reach Ophir Pass Road and the Chapman Gulch aid station number two at 10,160 feet and 18.6 miles.

"104, checking in."

The Essers and Stergius's are there to meet me. Walt has a big grin on his face.

"Way to go, Bob. It's 12:50. You're ten minutes ahead of your projected time. What can we get you?"

Pulling my Sport Vest over my head I'm pleased with myself.

"I feel great."

I've eaten all the food I was carrying-three Powergels, three GUs, four Powerbites, and a Cliff bar-and consumed all 80 ounces of my energy drink.

"Just dump my drop bag out and let's see what we have for lunch."

Sitting down on a lawn chair, Walt hands me a spaghetti and meatballs microwave meal. Judy and Helen are refilling my Sport Vest. I eat the microwave meals cold, but I don't have a vacuum for a mouth.

"Judy, can you give me my plastic spoon? It's in a sandwich bag in the large pocket on my vest."

"Here it is, Bob. I'm putting a peanut butter and honey sandwich in there along with all of these gels, GUs, and bars from your drop bag."

"Okay, thanks. Can you fill my bottle with half water and half Mountain Dew?"

"Sure thing."

Removing my previously white but now dirty and smelly shirt, I pull on a clean polypropolene jersey. I'll keep my Powerbar hat on. Walt hands me my vest. It's a little awkward to put it on when it is full of fluids, and my hat gets knocked off in the process. Walt and I wrestle each other to see who will fasten the snaps on each side. This is turning into a Laurel and Hardy comedy routine, but now I'm ready. I check to make sure my windbreaker is still attached to the vest.

"Thanks a lot, guys. See you in Telluride; 104, checking out." Next aid station: 9.4 miles.

It's 1:00 p.m., seven hours into the race. At 10:38, Karl Meltzer, 31, of Sandy, Utah, ran through Chapman's in first place two minutes ahead of Jan Fiala, 45, of Corrales, New Mexico. A pursuing pack of ten runners was eight minutes behind Karl, who won the 1998 Wasatch Front 100 miler in the record time of 20:08. Around 11:15, the three women-

Betsy Kalmeyer, Sue Johnston, and Betsy Nye-came through Chapman's within a minute or two of each other.

Heading up Ophir Pass Road, I'm joined by Joe, Ulli, Ballard, Roger Wiegand, and Rollin Perry. The course markings indicate we're supposed to turn left on Oscar's Pass Road, but Ulli and Roger, deep in conversation and oblivious of where they are going, hike right past them. This sort of thing happens even to people who know every inch of this course.

"Hey, guys, you missed the turn."

When the two errant runners rejoin us I fall in with Roger who is using ski poles

"Do the poles help you a lot, Rog?" I ask.

"They're a bother on the uphills, but give me more confidence on the downhills," Roger replies.

"I'm afraid that if I use them I'll trip and fall and end up jamming one of them up some bodily orifice." He seems to take the joke in stride.

"There's always the chance that you will get hurt."

Deciding to change the subject I ask, "Did you have a chance to get much high altitude training in before the race?

"We were out here a week before the race. Before that we spent about ten days in the Dolomites training at around 10,000 feet," Roger responds.

Dolomites? That stops me for a few seconds. I'm thinking, where the hell are the Dolomites? Over near Pagosa Springs? Then my many years of reading National Geographic magazine kick in.

"Oh, ya, Italy."

Conversation lags after this and I'm climbing stronger than Roger at this point so I move ahead. Actually, I notice that I have left everyone behind as I hike steadily up Oscar's Pass Road, which was built in the mid-1950's as a jeep road but is unused now. I'm breathing normally, I'm not taking any time out to stop and rest. In fact, it occurs to me that this is the best that I have ever climbed in my four years at this race or, for that matter, in my entire life, and it's happening on a punishing 2 1/2 mile uphill that gains over 2,600 feet of altitude and is generally feared by Hardrock runners. All the speed work sessions with Web Loudat and coming out to Colorado three weeks in advance are paying off for me.

A dozen switchbacks eventually bring me to the top of Oscar's Pass, the third of Hardrock's climbs at 13,120 feet. The sun is out and it's a beautiful day as I pause to survey Bridal Veil Basin spread out in a breathtaking panorama at my feet. Turning around, I marvel at the long distance view of Swamp Canyon and the terrain I have just crossed. Why do I keep entering this race? Just look around for the answer. Of course, the moments of exaltation are followed by hours of punishing toil.

The course flags direct me left onto a large snowfield. The snow is still frozen so I don't posthole but concentrate on putting my feet into the depressions made by previous runners and move quickly around the top of the basin. In previous years I found this situation — running across an icy snowfield at over 13,000 feet — totally exhausting, but today it's *"hakuna matata, bwana"*, *"no problemo, senor."*

The trick on this type of surface is to keep the feet moving. Approaching a section where the previous footsteps go up the icy slope, I make the mistake of slowing down, my feet go out from under me, and I plummet off the side of the mountain. A switchblade of adrenaline knifes through my body as I dig in my heels, elbows, and anything else that is sticking out to stop my involuntary glissade. Fortunately, the snowfield ends after fifty yards at some rocks. Otherwise, my fall would continue hundreds of feet down into the basin. Digging in slows me down enough so I don't injure myself when I hit the rocks. Surveying my situation I see that my destination, Wasatch Saddle, is above and to the right of my position. I decide not to try to climb back up the snowslick mountainside, but to take a detour around the snowfield on some rocks. This works out, and soon I'm back on the course at 13,060 feet, the top of Wasatch Saddle.

Another snowfield lies in front of me so I jump on for a downhill glissade into the Telluride Bear Creek drainage basin. Up until now the weather for the race has been perfect-partly cloudy skies and moderate temperature, but, like a woman's uncertain heart, the sky has darkened. Below me I can see that it is raining so at the bottom of the glissade I pause to put on my windbreaker and eat a GU. The trail here is a steep and treacherous downhill, lined with mean-looking rocks. If I slip and fall I can bust myself up. Two hikers have stopped below me and are sitting down to eat. I've never been a fan of wearing heavy hiking boots and lugging a sixty pound pack through the mountains and would rather keep moving through the night than try to sleep in a soggy tent.

It's raining now. These fellows look stoical as I approach.

"Hey guys, enjoying lunch?" I call out.

"Just a snack," one of them replies as I skip past.

Descending rapidly, I cross a meadow and plunge through the waters of the East Fork of Bear Creek. Wet feet are so much a part of this race that I don't give them a second thought. After crossing a hard snow field I pick up the Wasatch Trail and pass the remains of Nellie Mine on my left. So much snow is melting off the slopes higher up that the trail has become an ankle deep stream. After I cross a metal footbridge, the trail improves and soon I arrive at the intersection with Bear Creek Road. Turning left on this gravel road descent, I'm joined by Carl Yates who is wearing his usual floppy-brimmed hat and green running suit with long pants and long sleeved shirt. No matter how hot it gets, Carl wears his long pants to protect his legs from being cut and battered in falls. Of course, there's always the possibility that at 140 pounds Carl wears long pants because he doesn't want people to see how skinny his legs are. Last summer Carl entered seven of the most difficult 100 mile trail races to celebrate being 70. He isn't a big talker during the race. All his energy is focused on moving downhill as rapidly as he can, and he has developed a fantastic kind of loping stride where he reaches out as far as he can with one foot then follows with the other foot in a sort of giant walk down the road. It works for Carl and he pulls ahead of me.

We pass a middle age couple and I inform them, "That guy's 72 years old."

The woman startles me by replying, "You're no spring chicken yourself."

I don't have time to stop and offer her my thoughts on the relativity of the number of years a person has lived and its relation to that person's physical fitness level and mental outlook. Maybe some other time.

The road into Telluride is supposed to be two miles long. We have passed the place where the aid station is visible through the trees far below us. Eventually, we arrive at the sharp right turn onto a trail which takes us down to a soccer field and past a basketball court. I follow Carl over to the white tent-like structure where I check in and my crew is waiting for me. Elevation 8,750 feet, Telluride is aid station number three at the 28-mile point.

Walt's smile is as wide as ever.

"Hey, Bob, you're doing great. It's 4:30. You're a half hour ahead of your schedule. What can we get you?"

Wow, 4:30. I have been ignoring my watch so I'm stunned. Two years ago when I got here it was nearly 5:30 and I could tell from the looks on the faces of the crews that I was in trouble. Today, it's a different story.

We go through the same drill as we did at Chapman. It has stopped raining. Taking off my soggy windbreaker, I pull the vest over my head and give it to Judy to be filled again with energy drink and my other energy foods. Sitting down, I note "I guess it's time for an early supper. What's the microwave meal for this evening?"

Walt hands me beef stew with my plastic spoon. I need some fat.

"Can I have some chocolate milk?" I ask.

"Sure, Bob. Just a minute." Chocolate milk is something new I'm trying. I take a few swallows to wash down the beef stew.

Helen stands in front of me grinning.

"Anything else you need?"

I look down at my shoes. The velcro on my gaiters has been torn half open and they have crept up my ankles.

"Can you help me rearrange my gaiters?"

"Sure, Bob."

I work on one while she works on the other straightening and adjusting the gaiters, pulling them back down so they cover the tops of my shoes. I feel a little uncomfortable asking someone else to help me with my shoes. In my mind it's somehow demeaning to work on another person's shoes, maybe because when I was a 10 year old kid I shined shoes on Saturdays for customers at my Dad's barbershop for 50 cents a pair. The shine I put on the customer's shoes was never good enough for my Dad. He always had to give the shoes an extra buffing with the shine rag.

Thinking ahead, I realize it will be dark and cold before I see my crew again.

"Walt, do you have a blanket in your vehicle? I'll need one at Ouray so I don't get chilled sitting at the aid station."

"No, but we'll get one at the motel for you, Bob."

"Okay. Judy, can you somehow attach my black nylon pants to my vest. I'll need them tonight. And I want to wear my green Superior Trail 100 poncho." I'm proud of finishing the Superior Trail 100 in my home state of Minnesota.

"And I'll need one of my small flashlights too-the Garrity Life Lites. There should be one in my drop bag." It will be dark before I reach Ouray.

"Sure thing, Bob."

In a few minutes I'm ready to go, but the devotion of these people to helping me succeed in my quest suddenly overwhelms me and I break down emotionally. Pulling the bill of my cap down and ducking my head to hide the tears spilling down my face, I leave the aid station with Walt at my side.

"Sorry," I blubber; "I can't control my emotions." Living alone and raising my two kids as a single parent for twelve years, I grew used to doing everything for myself so I'm genuinely touched by the help I'm getting from my friends.

I'm also emotionally unsteady as a result of the physical effort I've put out over the past eleven hours.

Episodes such as this are like a naked cry from the heart. The process of running a 100 mile trail race strips us of our usual defense mechanisms and exposes our essence. Emotional and sometimes physical control is lost and our core identity is revealed. It's a scary but exhilarating experience.

Putting his arm around my shoulders Walt gives me a brotherly hug.

"That's all right, Bob. I'll walk you down to the bridge."

"Hey, wait a minute." I'm in a panic. "I forgot to check out. We've got to go back."

"Don't worry about it, Bob. I'll check out for you. Just go up here and take a right on Willow Street."

"Okay, Walt. Thanks for all your help." Next aid station: 5.3 miles.

After crossing the San Miguel River on a footbridge I turn right on Willow then cross Colorado Avenue, Telluride's main drag. Karl Meltzer came through town at 12:53 p.m., fifteen minutes ahead of his closest pursuers: Scott Gordon, 38, of Albuquerque, New Mexico, forty-two year old Dale Petersen of Denver, Colorado, and Kirk Apt, 37, of Crested Butte, Colorado. Kirk is a five-time Hardrock finisher and is usually among the top five finishers. Karl is 40 minutes ahead of Ricky Denesik and Blake Wood, 40, of Los Alamos, New Mexico. Blake's family-his Mom, Joyce, and Dad, Phil; wife, Rebecca; and his two daughters, Heather and Margaret-are crewing for him. Among the top women, Sue Johnston arrived in Telluride at 1:52 p.m., an hour behind Karl, and she was followed two minutes later by the two Betsy's.

I'm by myself hiking uphill on Liberty Basin jeep road north out of Telluride. It occurs to me that my tearful, emotional outpouring happened ten minutes after my feelings of joy when I learned that I was ahead of schedule entering the aid station. These exaggerated mood swings are common when I run 100 milers. One minute I'll be leaping and shouting like the wild man of Borneo, the next minute I'll be sunk in a deep Billie Holiday blues funk. I recover quickly, but in the process of running one of these races, I go through an entire year's worth of emotions in one or two days.

My destination is the next aid station at Virginius Pass. It's a 5.3-mile climb with an elevation gain of 4,350 feet, another of the hikes viewed with trepidation by Hardrock runners. I'm climbing easily and breathing normally. Two years ago I really struggled up this road.

Virginius Pass aid station. Photo by David Emory/HRH

Passing the pressure relief valve for the Telluride water supply reminds me of one of Charlie Thorn's favorite stories. In 1994, some of the volunteers who were helping at the Virginius Pass aid station were walking down this jeep road after dark when the relief valve went off, spouting water through a pipe next to the road. This is a noisy process and the volunteers thought they were hearing a bear roaring, so they decided to go no farther and spent a chilly night waiting for sunup when they realized their bear was just water erupting. Actually, I've heard the water being blown out of the pipe, and it doesn't sound anything like an animal noise, but I guess you had to have a vivid imagination and be there in 1994 to appreciate it.

The Heaphys must have beaten me out of Chapman aid station because I catch up with them again. I just say hi as I go by, not wanting to appear too pleased with myself since Margaret's knees seem to be bothering her. Further on I catch up to a runner who recognizes me.

"Hi, you're Bob, aren't you? I'm Rich Limacher." Rich, 49, is from Matteson, Illinois.

"Hey, Rich. How are you doing? Have you spoken to our friend in Georgia recently?"

"Sue Norwood? Yes, she's doing fine. I want to tell you that I enjoyed your book." Last year, Sue bought a copy of *Beyond the Marathon* as a gift for Rich before he did the Leadville 100.

"Thanks, I hope it gave you a few laughs."

"Yes, I enjoyed it. You should write another one."

"Well, you never know. I've been threatening to write one about this race for three years, but I've got to finish it first."

"You seem to be doing well today. Good luck to you."

"Thanks. I'll need it"

Moving ahead of Rich, I also leave the timberline behind. Upper Liberty Bell basin looms in front of me, rocky and steep. High above I can pick out runners laboring up the long dusty switchbacks. This is one of those "heed doon, arse oot" situations where you just work hard, pump your arms, suck down the fluids, and try not to think about how far you have to go or how long it's going to take. Now is the time to "become one with the mountain," as Ulli often suggests.

The *New York Times* tells me that Americans live in a sexually-charged, violent, technocratic society, but here I am peacefully hiking all alone at 13,000 feet in one of the least populated places in the U.S. without a machine in sight. I'm living in the now with no past and no future.

Reaching Mendota Saddle is my immediate goal. I can see it at the east end of the basin. Chug, chug, chug. Finally, I top out. Tongues of cloud drift over the surrounding peaks. The spectacular Marshall Basin drops hundreds of feet in front of me. This brief moment of exhilaration is the reward for my effort. I also derive simple satisfaction from the doing, the physical act of getting up here. It's all about rigor, ritual and repetition.

After pausing, I launch myself to my left onto a major snowfield. This is where I quit the race mentally two years ago. At that time I kept plunging through the surface of the snow, post holing up to my groin every step, and tearing up my ankles, shins, and knees on the knifelike edges of the icy crystals. Today, the snow is harder so I'm not sinking in, exhausting myself, and stopping to gasp for breath every ten feet. My heart rate is normal, not racing wildly. I'm acclimated and making decent time in the high country, not crawling along. Glancing up, I spot the three power poles on a bench in the distance that resemble the three crosses on Golgotha. Behind them I can see a blue tent that marks Virginius Pass, my next objective.

It's less than a mile through the snow around the top of Marshall Basin. Arriving at a steep gully just below the aid station, I use the technique of remaining upright and walking up the loose rock as quickly as I can. This works fine and contrasts sharply with my pitiful exhibition two years ago when I literally crawled up the gully on all fours and yelled for help when I didn't think I was going to make it.

Virginius Pass aid station number four, aka Kroger's Canteen, is at the top of significant climb number four. Kroger's Canteen, named after Chuck Kroger of Telluride, who originated and captains the aid station, is unique in 100-mile trail races and unbelievable until you climb up there and see it for yourself. It's situated in a small notch in St. Sophia Ridge at 13,100 feet. A tent has been set up along with several chairs, a gas stove, and a thick plastic sheet that cracks and strains at its moorings while protecting runners from the banshee winds that roar through the notch like a freight train. Chuck, Kathy Green, and several of their friends have carried all their gear plus water and food for 100 runners up here.

This is the site of the famous Rocket Rope glissade, the fastest 500 feet in trail utrarunning. In '97 when I peered over the edge of the cliff and got a load of the Rocket Rope, I couldn't believe my eyes and began interrogating the volunteers.

Bob: "Isn't there any other way off this mountain?"

Volunteer: "Not really."

Bob (thinking they must be lying, looking around wildly for their hidden vehicle): "Well, how did you get all this stuff up here?"

Volunteer: "We hiked just like you."

Bob (accepting his fate grudgingly): "Okay, give me some tea with double caffeine and double sugar."

Contrasting how good I feel today with how lousy I felt in '97 I again order tea with milk and sugar plus some mashed potatoes. It's 7:45 p.m. Karl Meltzer barely paused here when he flew through nearly five hours ago, still in the lead. Ulli and Ballard arrive while I'm waiting to have my order filled.

Ulli looks up at me, smiling. "Bob, this is the best I've ever seen you climb in this race."

"Thanks, Ulli. I'm going to finish this year."

The two companions don't waste much time here. A couple of other runners arrive. It's getting crowded in the notch, so they exit via the Rocket Rope. I'm next, but the young woman who has been bringing me my food grabs my arm and looks into my eyes. She wants to make sure I'm paying attention to what she is saying.

Runner preparing to descend the Rocket Rope at Virginius Pass. Photo by David Emory/HRH

Battling against the howl of the wind she shouts, "If you have any running pants you better put them on so you don't get torn up by the snow."

I've forgotten I'm carrying the nylon pants Judy tied to my vest.

"Can you get my pants? They're tied to the back of my pack."

I'm balancing on one foot to put on the pants as she holds my shoulder so I don't fall over. When this is done she yells at me.

"When you get to the end of the first glissade head for the right side of the notch. Do you see where I'm pointing?" Sighting down her arm, I pick up her point of reference.

"On the third glissade stay to the right of the rocks. Okay?"

"To the right of the rocks. All right. Thanks a lot. I'd love to hang around but gotta go." Next aid station: 3.2 miles.

Sitting down on the edge of the cliff I take the rope in my right hand, raise my left hand, and push off. This is the real Jetman, shooting like an express elevator down the nearly vertical slope, my feet raised so I don't snag something and start tumbling. The rope runs out. As I continue free falling somehow the water bottle that was attached to my Sport Vest comes loose and pops up into the air. I grab it so now I'm holding both hands in the air and only come to a stop when the slope levels out at a bench. What a rush.

"Thank you, Jesus." Only at Hardrock do runners have an experience of this intensity. And it's not over. This is a three-part glissade. Jogging over to the notch, I wait a moment for Ballard to reach the bottom then it's my turn. This slide isn't as thrilling as the first, but it's still a good ride down a slick groove in the snow made by a previous runner. Looking down at the third snowfield, I notice that Ulli and Ballard have gone to the left of the rocks. I distinctly remember the woman at the aid station telling me to stay to the right, so that's where I aim. Sailing past the rocks, I receive a rude shock as I plunge through the surface of the snow and come to an abrupt halt sitting in an ice-cold stream of water with snow up to my neck.

This is a new kind of fall-the snowsnake-where the frozen crust of snow gives way and down you go. Only at Hardrock. For a moment I can't figure out what to do, but I know I've got to get out of this water quickly so I twist my body and roll to my left. Reaching firm snow, I scoot on my butt to work up some speed and continue the glissade to the bottom of the gully where I lie still for a moment collecting my wits. I'm completely soaked but exhilarated, high on life.

Clambering to my feet, I stride across what Charlie calls a "parking lot" above the Virginius Mine site, where bulldozers have cleared buildings and created a level area. One hundred years ago miners worked here at over 12,000 feet throughout the long winter. Avalanches were a big problem so the miner's boarding houses at Virginius Mine were constructed hugging the walls of the basin with steep, reinforced roofs so the snow would slide over them.

A person caught in an avalanche is supposed to use a swimming motion to stay on top of the moving snow. That's easy to say, but avalanches are powerful forces of nature, hurtling down mountain sides at 100 miles per hour carrying huge boulders and giant trees. Once stopped, the ice and snow sets up like concrete and anyone buried deeply suffocates quickly. During the mining days, the only way searchers could locate avalanche victims was if a hand, head, or foot protruded from the snow. Otherwise people had to wait until the snow melted to recover the bodies and hold funerals. On one day, March 17, 1906, 21 men were killed and many others injured in snow slides in the Silverton district.

It's all downhill from the top of Virginius Pass to the town of Ouray, ten miles with a drop in elevation of 5,400 feet. My race plan calls for me to run this section which is all road from the mine to Ouray. As the gravel road descends along a ridge with Sidney Basin to the right and Governor Basin to the left, I'm not exactly running. I'm into what I call my high altitude shuffle which is more than a walk but less than a run. Breaking into my shuffle at this stage, not even close to the halfway point in the race, is not very impressive, but it's the best I can manage. It's not that my quads hurt; I've always had quads of steel. My problem is lack of leg speed.

It's still light out as I wade a stream flowing across a sharp bend in the switchbacking road. I can feel my toes rubbing against the front of my shoes. My feet must be swelling. Better change into larger shoes at Ouray. Don't want to invite blisters with many miles ahead of me.

Governor Basin aid station number five at 36.5 miles and 10,780 feet appears on my right. It's 8:50 p.m. I've been out here for nearly 15 hours and I've gone only 36.5 miles. That's what's so discouraging about this race. I'm killing myself on all these monster climbs and descents, and I'm going nowhere. Karl Meltzer ran through this aid station at 3:15 p.m. without even slowing down, twenty-five minutes ahead of Kirk Apt and Dale Petersen. Betsy Kalmeyer has taken the women's lead, an hour and a half behind Karl, but fifteen minutes ahead of Betsy Nye. I pause briefly to eat a banana, fill up my bottle with Coke and grab a handful of pretzels before pushing off. Next aid station: 7.2 miles.

The course follows Camp Bird Mine Road for seven miles past the ghost town of Sneffels, Camp Bird, and many other abandoned mines, all the way down to Ouray. Camp Bird Mine was owned by Thomas Walsh, who struck gold there in the 1890's. In 1899, 400 miners worked at Camp Bird. Their boarding house was a veritable palace, with flush toilets, electricity and a library. Later, Walsh sold the mine to a British syndicate for $6 million. His daughter, Evalyn Walsh, owned the Star of the East diamond and the Hope diamond. Many of the men who labored at his mine died young of silicosis or pneumonia or in avalanches or by their own hands and are buried in unmarked graves in these mountains.

I recall the last time I walked down Camp Bird Road, two years ago. I was in no particular hurry to get to Ouray because I planned to drop out there. The one event that made a positive impression on me that night was the moon rising over a cloud-shrouded peak in a way that made it look like the clouds were set ablaze by the moonlight. The fiery display only lasted for a few moments, but was absolutely stunning. Tonight the moon will rise late. The sky is partly cloudy. Some stars are out, but the road is in darkness.

The most impressive thing I'm doing this evening is peeing. I must have peed six times already. Each time I have to untie my nylon pants, pull them and my shorts down, try not to pee all over myself, pull everything back up, then tie my pants again. My body is getting rid of the excess fluids I pumped in during the daylight hours which is normal, but all the tying and untying is slowing me down.

With no moonlight, only the sound of rushing water fills the night on Camp Bird Road. At the intersection with the mine road, Sneffels Creek merges with Imogene Creek and becomes Canyon Creek on its urgent journey to the Uncompaghre River. During the day, tourists drive back and forth on Camp Bird Road making it a dusty passage, but only a few vehicles meet me tonight. I catch up with a runner standing on the side of the road fumbling with his butt pack. Turning my flashlight on him, I notice that he is wearing a Hinte-Anderson 50K race shirt.

"Hey, what's up? Don't you have a flashlight?"

"The batteries gave out. I've got some more in my pack."

I stop for a minute to give him some help with my light.

"I see you've done Hinte-Anderson. Are you an east coast guy?"

"Ya, I'm Harry Smith." Harry's from Manheim, Pennsylvania.

"I'm Bob from North Carolina. I've never done Hinte-Anderson. Maybe I'll get around to running it some day. It's kind of a long drive from North Carolina to Maryland just to do a 50K race."

"I know what you mean. Still it's a good race. You should try it." By now Harry has his light working as we swing down the road.

"I guess I'll have to put it on my list. Those must be the town lights up ahead. The Ouray turnoff can't be too far. It's a left turn onto a downhill trail. Should be well marked with ribbons. What they need here is a few chemlights." Harry quickens his pace leaving me to find the turnoff on my own.

I went over this part of the course on Wednesday, so it shouldn't hold any surprises. I recall Charlie's admonition that if I come to the high bridge over the Uncompaghre River, I have gone too far. Confusingly, some arrows pointing left have been spray painted on the pavement, but there is no trail here. Twenty yards further on, ribbons tied to some tree branches signal the turn.

As I descend a short way, my flashlight beam picks up a solid-looking stone building. In the past this was the explosive magazine for the Ouray mines. I find myself on Box Canyon Park Road, which brings me to the park itself, then to a bridge across the Uncompaghre River. On the other side of the bridge after a left turn I'm on Oak Street passing a trailer park on my right. This is where I joked with John DeWalt on Wednesday. I wonder how he's doing. I've got to pay attention at the end of the trailer park so as not to miss the right turn at the Ouray city repair shop. Two years ago I went straight past the turn and wound up on the northern outskirts of town an hour later. I was dropping out anyway so it didn't make any difference, but bungling the turn was still aggravating. Tonight I'm still in the race, so I don't want to screw up. The repair shop comes into view, I make my turn and course ribbons take me across the Uncompaghre on a cable bridge. Traversing this springy contraption is like walking on a trampoline.

A right turn brings me to the Ouray town park where aid station number six is situated at the 43.7 mile point, 7,680 feet, the lowest elevation on the course. Helen and John are here to meet me.

"Hey, guys. Thanks for being here. Where are the Essers?"

"They're back at the motel getting some sleep. Here's your blanket and stool if you want to sit down. It's 11:00. What else can we get you?"

11:00! Crap. My heart sinks. The 48 hour pace time at this aid station is 11:30. I wanted to arrive in Ouray by 10:30 so I would have an hour cushion. At this rate I'm just barely staying ahead of the pace that will allow me to finish the race in the time allowed.

"I'm going to change almost everything here-shoes and socks, I'll need my orange polypro shirt, my black fleece pants, and my Redskins knit cap."

The Stergius's go to work. John rummages through my clothing bag while Helen pulls off my shoes.

"John, I'm going to wear my Montrail shoes. They've already got the gaiters attached. Where's my drop bag? I need my microwave meal." The Montrails are size 13, too big by half a size even if my feet are swollen, but they worked well for me during training and their reinforced toe box should protect my feet during the second half of the race when I will be tired and clumsy and prone to kicking rocks instead of stepping over them.

Joe Riddle arrives at the aid station. Apparently, his crew isn't here.

"Has anyone seen a VW bus?" Joe asks. Nobody responds. If it were me I would be throwing a fit jumping up and down and screaming, but Joe stays calm.

"What about drop bags? Where are the drop bags?" he begs plaintively

I wish I could help Joe, but I've got to take care of my own business. First, open up my bean soup microwave meal. This should make my bowels move. In the winter Ouray is an ice climbing mecca. It's hard to tell how cold it will be tonight, but I don't want to take any chances with hypothermia.

"I want to wear my blue vest and my gore-tex jacket. Let me put on these pants. They should keep my legs warm. I'll just pull them on over my shorts. Are the stars out? If we have cloud cover, it won't be too cold, but if the sky is clear the temperature will drop. I don't want to freeze my butt."

"Looks like we've got some stars, Bob," Helen responds. "I put your peanut butter and honey sandwich in your vest pocket." I've been religiously eating my sandwiches at every aid station. Being able to swallow the bread has surprised me. Usually, anything dry like bread gets stuck halfway down my throat and I wind up retching and spitting it out, but today I'm doing fine. I need the fat and the calories.

Helen asks, "What about flashlights, Bob? Do you have yours?"

"Yes, I'm keeping the Garrity Life Lite I was using on Camp Bird Road, and I've got another one in my jacket pocket plus a more powerful one if we need a strong beam. I don't think we will, but it's good to have just in case. Does John have his lights?"

"Yes," John replies, "I'm ready to go. Do you want to take your water bottle along?"

"No, I won't need it. I'm already peeing every five minutes. We've got an aid station between here and Grouse Gulch so I can fill my vest there if I'm running short of fluids. I guess that's it. Thanks, Helen. See you tomorrow."

Next aid station: 8.2 miles.

Karl Meltzer arrived at Ouray at 4:30 p.m., a half hour ahead of Kirk Apt and Dale Petersen, who have teamed up. Psychologically it's easier to do a 100 mile race with a partner than alone even if you don't talk much. Just the presence of another person is reassuring, and you can feed off each other's energy. Most of the time at Hardrock the winning runners will have top quality pacers who are also excellent trail runners, and this will give them an edge over those who do not have pacers.

Ouray is the first aid station where Karl Meltzer stops for any length of time-eight minutes. Blake Wood is in 11th place, a whole hour behind Karl, but 30 minutes ahead of his 1997 time at Ouray, when he completed the race in 33:43.

This year Blake hopes to match his '97 finish and figures he has a 50% chance of improving on it. He picks up his pacer, Igor Pesenson, an undergrad at the University of California/Berkely, who spends his summers working with Blake at the Los Alamos National Laboratory.

Betsy Kalmeyer gets into Ouray at 6:00 p.m., fifteen minutes ahead of her competition. Her crew (Dick Curtis and Julie and Duane Arter) is keeping her up to date on where the other women are in the race. They are all experienced trail runners. Dick has finished Hardrock and Julie has been first woman at Leadville. Besides crewing they will take turns pacing her. This evening Julie follows Betsy out of Ouray aid station.

If you are not having a good day, Ouray is a convenient place to drop out since it is a major aid station with crew access. Last year's winner, Ricky Denesik, calls it quits here today having twisted his knee in the snow back on Grant-Swamp Pass.

John and I trot out of the park past the gazebo and find our way to Second Street. All the people in these houses are fast asleep. We have a nine mile climb ahead of us through the night.

"I hate being under the gun like this, having to worry constantly about not making the 48 hour cutoff time," I confess to John. "It takes all the enjoyment out of the race. I wish just once that I could be at least in the middle of the pack and not at the back of the pack."

"Make sure you eat your sandwich," John replies.

"I'm talking about time, John. Not sandwiches." I'm getting a little testy.

"Ya, but if you don't eat your sandwich you won't have the energy to even make the 48 hour cutoff." John is a realist. I dutifully dig into my vest pocket, retrieve my sandwich from its baggy, and commence chomping.

Taking a right turn at the Best Western Motel, we return to Box Canyon Road and retrace my earlier steps past the old explosives magazine and climb up onto Camp Bird Road. A few hundred yards up Camp Bird, we turn left onto Dam Road, an unused jeep road that funnels us past the large pipe used to bring water to Ouray. On Wednesday when I was reconnoitering this section, I walked on top of the pipe to get past four steel cables that connect the pipe to some rocks preventing it from falling 100 feet into the river gorge. Tonight I play it safe, stay on the ground, and clamber over the waist high cables.

After negotiating a slippery up and down trail section, we arrive at the Uncompaghre River crossing. Runners and pacers are lined up to ford the river so we have to wait our turn.

John tells me, "When we were waiting for you at the aid station I overheard some pacers telling their runners they would meet them at the highway so they wouldn't have to get their feet wet here."

I can't believe this.

"What the hell are they doing pacing at Hardrock if they're afraid of getting their feet wet, for God's sake. They're in for a rude shock if they think their tootsies are going to stay dry on this course."

The runners ahead of us quickly cross the river; then it's our turn. Taking hold of the rope I step in the cold water. As I slide step across the river, the water rises above my knees, but the current isn't too bad. Emerging from the baptism of my fresh shoes, we follow a trail up to the original Ouray to Silverton toll road, built by Otto Mears a century ago. After a short stint on Otto's road, we climb up the cliff to the south end of the Highway 550 tunnel, the start of the Bear Creek National Recreation Trail.

Otto Mears was a Russia-born orphan who immigrated to the United States as a child and spent his adulthood in the late 19th and early 20th centuries building roads and railroads in the San Juan Mountains. His construction career began in the 1870's when he built a toll road into Lake City from the east; then he secured a contract to deliver mail from Lake City to Ouray, a 70-mile journey which took three days on foot in the winter. After completing the Ouray to Silverton toll road in 1884, he turned his attention to assembling the Rio Grande Southern Railroad, linking Ridgeway with Telluride in 1890. In extending the Rio Grande Southern from Telluride to Durango, he created an engineering marvel hanging rails on narrow shelves hundreds of feet above canyons and tossing trestles over deep gorges.

The trail takes us up and over the top of the tunnel, and we continue east with me in the lead. This trail provides hikers with outstanding views and dramatic drops of 400 feet into the canyon during daylight hours, but as Charlie said during the long briefing, "Acrophobia, exposure, yada yada yada. It'll be dark so you won't see the dropoff anyway."

The bottom section of Bear Creek Trail is all switchbacks. As we climb, I'm looking for my favorite tree: a gigantic, ancient Douglas fir tree that grows at an angle right on the trail; its huge limbs reach out to shelter all who pass under it. It's the only tree I've ever wanted to hug, but its trunk is probably fifteen feet in circumference, so my arms are too short to go all the way around. Here it is in my flashlight beam.

"Hi, pal." I pat its limb as we pass by. "Wish me well tonight."

In the same vicinity the trail crisscrosses a huge shale field. Walking across the shale produces a clanking sound like crunching crockery. In the years when the course goes counter-clockwise, the unusual noise made by footsteps on the shale is a welcome sound because it announces that runners are near the bottom of the trail. Tonight it just means I have a five mile trudge ahead of me in the wee hours of the morning.

Portions of the trail have been blasted out of the rock. Sensing the exposure, I instinctively lean to my left, hugging the canyon wall for fear of falling off the trail into the abyss. As predicted, we get our feet wet several times wading streams coming from our left and feeding into Bear Creek, roaring in the canyon far below us. With Helen and John last

Sunday, we could see the openings of mine shafts that had been dug into sheer sidewalls on the other side of the canyon. We wondered how the miners were able to reach the outcroppings since the side of the canyon is vertical and there seems to be no way of accessing the mine mouths, to say nothing of working the mines. Even though they committed environmental mayhem, the engineering skills of the people working at this altitude in all kinds of weather were phenomenal.

On our side of the canyon we pass the ruins of two mines, Grizzly Bear Mine and Yellow Jacket Mine. Casting my flashlight beam to the right of the trail, I shine it on a large, cylindrical cast iron container that looks like a boiler. Marveling at its presence here beside this mountain footpath, I make the obvious observation.

"That thing must weigh a ton. How the hell do you think they got it up here?"

"Well, it's a cinch they didn't bring it up on this trail. Probably came down from Engineer Pass on a road. This place is like an open air museum with all this old mining equipment lying around," John replies.

We lapse into silence. John is a taciturn guy. If I don't ask him a question, he keeps quiet. I occupy myself with closely examining the trail edge to see if I can pinpoint the place where I stepped into space last year and sprained my ankle. It's hard to tell in the dark.

Plodding up the trail thinking about that long night last year and the disappointment of dropping out of the race after I was injured, my attitude downshifts into low gear. I'm running like a bureaucrat. Just once I'd like to be up front among the cheetahs, duking it out, in the thick of things, instead of plugging along bringing up the rear like a wounded rhinocerous. Whine, whine.

This endless slog in total darkness except for a small flashlight beam is driving me into the doldrums. All day I was on a winning roll. Blasting up those climbs. Hurtling down those descents. Now loser images have taken over my

116

thoughts. Order is giving way to randomness. The idea of giving up enters my mind. I never voice my thoughts to John, but I've sunk into dreary despondency. I'm miserable. My legs are moving mechanically of their own accord. Suddenly I trip on something and fall flat on my face like a load of cement. It's a classic "hidden rock" fall. Pain shoots through my left hand. I lay there in the cold, soggy mud for a few moments.

"Aw shit," is all I have to say.

"Are you gonna get up?" John asks.

"Dunno," I reply. "Maybe."

Clutching my hurting finger with my other hand makes it feel a little better. All the jolly fun has drained out of this little adventure. Sighing, death-haunted, I struggle to my feet and resume the march. If this was Bataan in 1942 I would have dropped out by now and gotten my head smashed in.

All my senses are straining, searching for the next aid station. I'm seeking any suggestion of the warm glow of a campfire through the trees, any hint of the welcoming sound of voices in the distance. But nothing turns up. All we need is a steady drizzle to complete this gloomy picture, but actually it's a nice starry night, not as cold as I thought it would be. We pass by a Forest Service sign. The trail on our right will take us to Engineer Pass.

"Is that a campfire ahead of us, John?" I ask hopefully.

"No. You must be hallucinating," he replies unhelpfully.

"You know, last year Hans van Willigen hallucinated that he was seeing condo apartments during the climb up to Virginius Pass. That was in daylight. A couple of years ago I saw horses and riders ahead of me at the Massanutten race. When I reached the place where I saw them they had vanished into thin air."

After negotiating a frozen snowfield, we climb up through a grove of spruce. Finally, a yellow glow flickers through the limbs of the trees. Engineer, aid station number seven, comes into view: 11,480 feet, 51.9 miles, just past the half way point. It's 3:30 a.m.

117

"Number please," one of the volunteers asks.

"Oh, ya," I've forgotten that I'm wearing my gore-tex jacket over my vest so my number is covered up. "Sorry, it's 104. And this is my pacer. You guys got any potato soup?"

We move away from the campfire over to the cooking area that is protected by a sheet of plastic tied to some trees.

"We're running short of everything. They told us to expect around 70 runners, but we've had over 100 pass through here tonight," a volunteer informs us. "We don't have any clean cups."

I reach down and pick one up off the ground.

"Here's a cup. Can I have some potato soup?" Hey, this is Hardrock. The last thing I care about at this point is whether my soup cup is clean or not. The aid station version of potato soup turns out to be warm water with instant potatoes stirred in. The fact that it tastes like shredded cardboard doesn't bother me either. I never complain about aid station service. It's the middle of the night and these people carried all this stuff down here from Engineer pass road so anything they improvise is fine with me.

"Okay, thanks a lot. Ready to go, John? We're out of here. Number 104 and pacer are leaving." Next aid station: 7.3 miles.

Karl Meltzer passed through Engineer aid station at 7:14 p.m. without pausing. Kirk Apt and Dale Petersen were twenty minutes behind him. Randy Isler, 42, of Tijeras, New Mexico, is a half hour behind Kirk and Dale. Randy is closely followed by Hans Put, 38, from New York; Curtis Anderson, 36, Karl's running buddy from Sandy, Utah; and James Nelson, 38, from Layton , Utah.

Randy Isler is a three-time Hardrock finisher, all in the top five, who keeps in shape by rock climbing in New Mexico. He acclimates for Hardrock by camping at Ophir Pass (12,000 ft.) for two weeks before the race. In the past he has gone out too fast, but today he is hanging back and biding his time. Or maybe he just can't keep up with Karl. Hans Put is German. This is his first time at Hardrock. Nelson and

Anderson have both finished Wasatch in under 24 hours. Betsy Kalmeyer came through Engineer at 8:55 p.m., fifteen minutes ahead of Sue Johnston, who was five minutes ahead of Betsy Nye.

Pounding up the trail I feel a little better.

"It's a couple of miles to Engineer Pass," I inform John, "and over a thousand feet of climb."

Scuttling out from under the shelter of the forest we splash through a couple of the ubiquitous streams on the course. Our flashlight beams pick up the reflective flag markers, and we can see the flashlights of a half dozen runners ahead of us working their way up to the pass. Turning around, I see two lights behind us that are up high, as if giants holding flashlights are pursuing us. Spooky. It's a nighttime visual delusion created by runners wearing headlamps. It's still too dark to see Engineer Mountain in front of us, but suddenly a bright light pops up over the crest of a ridge to our left.

"What in the world is that?" I ask John. It looks so close-maybe half a mile away. "Are those car headlights?" To my knowledge there is no road to our left, but what else could it be?

"Wow, it's really bright." As we proceed uphill the light elongates. "This is really weird." Then John figures it out.

"It's the moon," he announces. Less than a quarter of the moon is illuminated. That's why it looked so strange rising. There's always something unexpected at night in the high country.

"Last year when Walt was pacing me, we walked up Engineers Pass Road at night under a full moon. The moonlight reflecting off the peaks and the snowfields was really spectacular," I tell John.

As we follow the trail upward, Ulli joins us from the darkness off to the left.

"Where did you come from?" I inquire.

"I've been having a little bit of trouble with my stomach so I was relieving myself," he replies.

John says, "There's supposed to be a blinking red light at the top of the pass-one of those bicycle rear seat lights. Do you see it?"

"Not yet. It should come into view soon." Ulli stays just ahead of us.

I'm not interested in red lights. My gaze is directed straight ahead to pick out the marking flags.

"There it is." Ulli reports. A red light is flashing above and ahead of us.

"It's better to follow this trail here to the right," Ulli says. "Going straight up to the light is too steep."

"Whatever you say, chief. Lead the way." We follow Ulli. This trail is steep enough for me.

We arrive at Engineer Pass Road (12,910 ft), the apex of climb number five, near the oddly named Oh! Point. I've been carrying a flare I had stashed in my drop bag at Ouray. The plan is to shoot it off to celebrate topping out at Engineer Pass.

"Have you ever shot off a flare?" I ask John. Being a military man I figured he would have some experience in this area.

"Sure, why?" he responds.

"I've got one here." I hand it to him. "I want you to shoot it back over the trail we just climbed. It will give the other runners a cheap thrill," says Mr. Excitement Himself.

John is fiddling around with the flare.

"Shine your light over here," he says.

It's a Skyblazer XLT model sold mainly to boaters. The directions are simple: Press top-flare will drop down; pull down to lock; unscrew cap; hold above head away from face-pull chain to launch.

"I don't want to shoot it back where we came from," John says. "The others will think it's some kind of emergency signal."

"Okay. Shoot it out in front of us. No one will see it except us."

"All right. Here goes."

With that John holds the flare above his head, pulls the cord and the flare ignites, arcing up and out sizzling red over the side of the road for maybe ten seconds before it winks out.

"I say, good show, old bean. Good clean fun." The flare caper has rejuvenated me. I feel like a naughty first grader waggling his tongue behind teacher's back. With the North Star pushing us, we stride along Engineer Pass Road at a brisk walk, heading for Animas Forks. Years ago miners carved this road out of the side of Engineer Mountain, which, like every other mountain around here, is absolutely honeycombed with abandoned mines. Dawn comes silently. The sky lightens as John and I descend, quick marching around switchbacks, swinging our arms. The Bridge on the River Kwai song enters my mind and I whistle it for a while.

A small voice in the back of my mind tells me that my race masterplan called for me to run this long downhill, but I'm content with a powerwalk. I'm making decent time and I don't want to exhaust myself just before the major climb to the top of Handies Peak. Should I be running? Probably. Such decisions make the difference between success and failure at Hardrock.

We cross the Denver Bridge that isn't far from Denver Lake, Denver Pass, and Denver Hill. I begin to notice that John is bumping into me from time to time. Checking to make sure that I'm walking in a straight line I inquire,

"Doing a little angle walking, John?"

"Huh?"

"I say, with all these rocks in the road, it's hard not to bump into each other."

"Oh, ya." Not a talkative fellow, our John.

The bean soup that I ate at Ouray is finally having its way with my bowels.

"John, I've got to take a dump." We're still well above tree line.

"There's no place around here to take one."

"I'll just have to improvise because there's no way I'm going to hold this until we reach someplace better."

Departing from the road, I step into a gully eroded by snowmelt and head downhill 50 feet. I don't want to stink up the joint too badly. Removing the toilet paper from its sandwich bag, I pull down my pants, squat and release. A major buildup of excreta flows onto the tundra. What a relief. Using plenty of t.p., I wipe carefully. Don't want to get any on my gloves. All finished. Pants up, I return to the serious business of running these one hundred miles.

Off we go marching to Pretoria. In my mind I remember Charlie's directions at the briefing for this stretch of road-follow the signs for Animas Forks and for Silverton. Don't go uphill. I can do this.

After a while I notice that John is weaving all over the place. Maybe he's playing games, I think. He trips, staggers and almost falls down. Odd behavior. Then it dawns on me. He's falling asleep on his feet.

"Hey, John. Doing all right, buddy?"

"Ya, I'm okay." John is pooped out after getting only a few hours of sleep on Thursday night then staying awake this past night with me.

I'm wide awake. It's been light enough to see without a flashlight for half an hour. The ghost town buildings of Animas Forks are visible to our right.

"Hey, John. Animas Forks coming up."

We catch up with Californian Michael Soltesz. Maybe between the two of us we can keep John awake until we reach the aid station.

"Hey, pal. How're ya doin?" I ask.

"I'm bonking. I can hardly keep my eyes open," Michael responds.

This is great. Now I've got two guys falling asleep on me. Time to wake them up with a joke.

"I've got a true story for you guys. You know that this summer is the 30th anniversary of Neil Armstrong's landing on the moon. You recall Neil's famous words when he first set foot on the lunar surface, 'That's one small step for man, one giant leap for mankind'? Well, when he was leaving the moon he said something else that has puzzled NASA officials and scholars ever since. He said, 'Good luck, Mr. Gorske.' When he got back to earth, people in the space program wanted to know what he meant by that, but he refused to tell them. People in the CIA thought it might have been some secret code for the Soviets, but they couldn't find a Mr. Gorske who worked for the Russians or anyone else. Reporters wanted to ask Neil about Mr. Gorske, but he rarely gave interviews until last month in Houston when he finally agreed to discuss his famous statement.

"At his press conference Neil said, 'Everyone affected by my words is dead now, so at long last I can reveal what I meant when I was on the moon and said "Good luck, Mr. Gorske." When I was a little kid, the Gorskes were our next door neighbors. We used to play baseball in their yard. One day I was playing the outfield when one of my buddies hit a long fly ball that landed right under the Gorske's bedroom window. I was scared to go get it, but I had to so I crawled over there. When I picked up the ball I heard Mrs. Gorske yell, "ORAL SEX, ORAL SEX, ALL YOU WANT IS ORAL SEX. I'LL GIVE YOU ORAL SEX WHEN THE KID NEXT DOOR WALKS ON THE MOON." ' "

Michael snorts, but John doesn't say anything. Animas Forks consists of a couple of log buildings from the 1920's on our right and the remains of a mine mill, looking like huge concrete steps climbing up the mountainside, on our left. Also on our left is the Alpine Loop road to Cinnamon Pass and Sherman, the next aid station after Grouse Gulch.

Soon the aid station comes into view. As we arrive I tell John, "You know, I quit a hundred times in my mind during the night, but thanks to you we made it this far."

John seems puzzled by my revelation. "I was just trying to stay awake," he says.

Grouse Gulch, aid station number eight: the 59.2 mile point in the race at 10,710 feet. It is located in the Animas

River valley, a spectacular corridor lined on both sides with 13,000 foot high mountain peaks. Michael has dropped back. We can see vehicles parked along both sides of the road and two white structures, one a tent and the other a round yurt. It takes us a few more minutes before we cross the bridge over the Animas River and arrive. The Essers' Jeep Cherokee is parked next to the yurt, so I call out my number to the volunteers, "104 and pacer checking in," and walk over to their vehicle. As usual, Judy and Walt are glad to see us.

"Right on time, Bob. Just like clockwork. It's 6:45. You're fifteen minutes ahead of the 48 hour cutoff. What can I getcha?" I've taken off my gore-tex jacket and Sport Vest for refilling.

"How bout a blanket?" Standing still for a just few minutes has brought on shivering.

"Sure thing. Here's your breakfast." It's a ham and scalloped potatoes microwave meal. My favorite. By now my crew knows its job, so all I have to do is sit and eat and think. What should I wear for this next section? I'm cold now. Handies is next. It's a fourteener, so it will be a cold and windy climb. On the other hand, I'll be coming off Handies and on the road into Sherman at mid-day and it will probably be warm. Reviewing the clothes I have in my bag and the certainty that I have another day and another night ahead of me-and the fact that I want to stay warm and can always take clothes off if I'm too warm-I decide not to change anything, just continue wearing my gore-tex jacket and fleece pants. The simplest solutions are the best. On second thought, I'm going to exchange my Redskins knit hat for my green Hardrock billed cap.

"All right then, I'm ready to go. Thanks, guys; 104 checking out." Next aid station: 10.9 miles.

I'm on my own again. It feels strange to be leaving John behind. He's standing by the Jeep looking weary. I'll see him again early tomorrow morning.

Grouse Gulch is a convenient place to drop out. I should know. That's where I quit in 1996, my first year at Hardrock.

It's close to Silverton's hot showers and warm beds. Today a dozen runners hand in their ID bracelets. At 9:17 p.m. Karl Meltzer arrived at Grouse Gulch, still number one. He left twelve minutes later. Kirk Apt had Karl in sight all the way down Engineer Pass Road, pulled into the aid station two minutes behind him. Dale Petersen is five minutes behind Kirk. After attending to their needs, Karl, Kirk, and Dale head up the Grouse Gulch trail together. Hans, Randy, and Curtis are half an hour behind the leaders, and Blake Wood is a whole hour behind. Although it's after dark, Blake drops his pacer here concerned that the inexperienced Igor might have problems negotiating the treacherous descent from Handies Peak.

Betsy Kalmeyer got to Grouse Gulch at 10:54 p.m. She was followed at 11:31 by Sue Johnston, with Betsy Nye right behind her. With forty miles ahead of her and facing the arduous trek to the top of Handies, Sue elected to spend only a few minutes at the aid station. Betsy Nye spent sixteen minutes fueling up.

In order to connect with the course, I have to retrace my steps a couple of hundred yards on Engineer Pass Road from Walt's vehicle to the place where a marking flag signals a right turn onto an abandoned jeep road snaking up the side of Cinnamon Mountain. Climbing steadily up a series of switchbacks with a stream downhill on my right, I warm up and stop shivering. Spotting two figures ahead of me, I decide to try to catch them.

This is all above treeline and in shadow because I'm heading east and the sun is shielded by the top of the ridge in front of me. Continuing uphill through the hanging valley that is Grouse Gulch, I arrive at a grassy saddle where the sun greets me. Swinging around to my left I encounter some campers who have pitched their tents in a glacial valley. Several of them are standing around; one is lying in her sleeping bag in the sun warming up after a cold night. The course markers take me behind their tents. I wave at them, but don't say anything. Soon I climb to the ridge that is the

American-Grouse Pass, the top of climb number 6, at 13,020 feet. The two guys I have been chasing are up here talking to a woman I hadn't seen before. I can't tell if the men are in the race or are just day hikers. The woman speaks to me.

"Don't forget to punch your number at Sloan Lake."

"Gotcha."

I haven't forgotten. Who is this woman? Is she a race official? What are these people doing up here? I have no idea and am not about to stop and inquire. Handies Peak is directly in front of me on the other side of American Basin. Below me is a huge snowfield that I'll have to glisssade in order to reach Sloan Lake at the bottom of the basin. I don't see any way to hike around this snowbank, but I'm scared because from where I am, I can't see the bottom of the hill. I don't want to just jump off the top without being able to see where I'm going since there might be rocks below or some sheer dropoff. I can see myself soaring into space and landing on my head hundreds of feet below. It doesn't occur to me that if this was a dangerous place, Charlie would have said something about it at the briefing. I'm in self-preservation mode, and I don't want to mess up my chances of finishing because I get injured.

Inching out on the slippery snow to the edge of the hillside, I see the buttmarks that have been made by previous glissaders. No rocks rise up to maim me. Happily, I slide the several hundred feet down to the bottom of the basin. Picking up the trail markers, I cross a stream that must be the Lake Fork of the Gunnison River. The basin is a spectacular place surrounded by rugged peaks and ridges. Many hikers come up here to bag Handies. Looking up from the trail, I spot two large elk with full sets of antlers galloping off to my right. It's odd to see just two male elk together like this. The rest of the herd must be hiding somewhere.

I'm concentrating now on finding Sloan Lake and the famous punch. Charlie said it would be attached to an orange and white orienteering flag and sitting on a cairn. Shouldn't be too hard to locate, but several puddles of melted snow litter the bottom of the basin, and I have no idea which one of them is Sloan Lake. This trail was built three years ago to discourage people from bushwhacking to the top of Handies. The more direct routes were tearing up the tundra. The result is a trail that meanders across meadows and through streams and switchbacks up and down ridges and passes numerous piles of rocks alongside various ponds that may or may not be Sloan Lake. Putting a punch on the trail is Charlie's way of keeping us off the direct approach through the tundra.

By this time I am certain that I have somehow missed the punch, but I'll be damned if I'm going back to look for it. Race officials will just have to take my word for it that I stayed on the stupid trail. What if some righteous hiker didn't like the alien orange and white flag spoiling the natural grandeur of one of America's beauty spots and removed it, punch and all? What if it was trampled by a herd of elk? I'm getting pretty gol-darned worked up about this whole punch thing when low and behold the apparatus appears on top of its cairn just where it's supposed to be. Thank the Lord for small favors.

From here the trail angles down through some nasty slide rock and across a couple of snowfields before it begins the climb to the top of Handies. Ascending the switchbacks I spot two figures below me who are catching up. They turn out to be Roger Wiegand and his wife, Sylvia, who is pacing him. Sylvia is wearing a green bonnet.

"What a fine bonnet. Are you Amish?" I inquire. Sylvia is amused.

"No, it's for the sun."

The sun dazzles at this altitude. I'm wearing sunglasses and have pulled the bill of my hat down over my eyes. We arrive at the saddle just south of the summit, and the Wiegands push ahead of me. Roger is climbing well. Up here the earth is rocky. Tiny wild flowers hug the ground, all their energy devoted to growing long roots to search for water rather than to stem growth. As I stagger to the top, a couple passes me on their way down. The man is carrying a sleeping infant.

"How old is your baby?" I ask.

"He's three months."

I can feel the altitude up here. I'm wheezing. My lungs hurt. A powerful wind is hammering me. Is it wise to bring a baby up this high?

"Well, he's going to have a heck of a cardio-vascular system when he grows up," is all I say to these people.

Sylvia and Roger Wiegand near the top of Handies Peak. Photo by Bob Boeder

The cone-shaped summit of Handies Peak: the 64.5 mile point, 14,048 feet, the high point on the course, and the end of significant climb number seven. Four or five people-day hikers-are at the top when I get there. The Wiegands haven't wasted any time at the summit and are heading down. Since I have invested all this energy getting here, I want to sign the Colorado Mountain Club register to make it official. Some guy wearing heavy hiking boots and a large backpack is eager to help me, so he unscrews the pipe container and removes the register and pen from inside. Fourteen thousand plus feet of altitude is no place for precision watch repair. I'm shaking so badly that I can barely scribble my name, the date, and "HRH #104" under remarks.

Time to get out of here. I remind myself to stay strong on the next section of the course. This is where I quit mentally in both 1996 and 1998. Those were counterclockwise course years, so I was ascending. Today, I'm going down. The way to travel between Handies and Sherman aid station has changed several times since 1992. The first two years the course took runners northeast down into Grizzly Basin then followed Grizzly Gulch to Cinnamon Pass Road. From there it was five road miles to the aid station. In Charlie's zeal to make Hardrock as much of a trail race as humanly possible, in 1994 the course was changed to a southeasterly trail into Boulder Basin and Gulch, ending up on Cottonwood jeep road. From there it's two miles to the aid station.

In 1998 Charlie came up with a variation on the Boulder Basin route. It's not on any map, but John Cappis coined the quaint moniker, Up-Chuck Ridge, to honor Charlie for his discovery. It's yet to come. First, there's another punch up here to mark my number. I don't have to search for this one. Not far from the summit the course angles left under a protective overhang, and I discover it attached to an orange and white flag. It's pleasantly warm here out of the wind, but I don't linger. Carl Yates has caught up with me and wants to punch his number, so I proceed on the ridgetop trail. Grizzly Gulch lies at the bottom of a 1000-foot drop on my left, with

Boulder Gulch the same distance down to my right. Last year a lightning and hail storm pinned down some runners on this exposed ridge, frightening them badly. There's some evidence that a lightning strike within a few feet of a person can cause a heart attack even without the electric current entering the body. Today we're lucky and the weather is fine.

This terrain calls for the utmost concentration on foot placement while not losing sight of the markers. I'm looking for Charlie's candidate for the most dangerous part of the course. It takes longer than I thought it would to reach, but finally I arrive at a rock outcropping that prevents me from descending any further on the ridge. To my right a steep gully points hundreds of feet down into Boulder Gulch. If I lose my footing and fall here there's nothing to stop me until I reach the bottom of the gulch. Breathing heavily, I inch my way down the gully on loose rock, hugging the wall around the base of the outcrop, moving from handgrip to handgrip until I reach a faint animal trail which continues along the west side of the ridge. Thankful for having made it safely this far, I'm faced with going down a steep grassy slope 550 feet to the bottom of the gulch. Narrow terraces have been created by animals moving along the slope. These provide occasional flat places for footholds, but it is so steep I have to go down on my backside. Trying to walk down is impossible, providing only an invitation to fall. Behind me I hear Carl grunt as his legs go out from under him.

I yell, "Are you all right, Carl?"

Either he can't hear me in the wind or he chooses to ignore me. I watch as Carl gets up and tries again, this time feet first on all fours in a kind of downhill reverse crawl. I can see he hasn't been hurt. I'm concerned about Carl and would do anything for him although I realize he expects nothing from me.

Last year I literally had to crawl on all fours up this slope and the effort it required was so extreme that it killed any interest I had in continuing the race. Today's descent is like sliding sideways down a wall with occasional footholds. I can see Roger and Sylvia have reached the bottom. I hate the time it is taking to get off this mountain. Eventually, I bottom out. Proceeding southeast across Boulder Gulch stream, I look up. Square Gulch lies directly in front of me on the other side of Cottonwood Canyon. Entering the trees, I catch up to and pass two runners who seem unhappy with each other.

Beyond "hey guys" I have nothing to say to them and continue downhill until I reach Cottonwood Creek jeep road. The sun is hammering me out of a cloudless sky. I should run the two miles to the aid station but settle for a brisk walk. I'm carrying my gore-tex jacket, but I'm still wearing my fleece pants. I don't want to overheat and get dehydrated at this point in the race. Again, small decisions like this can make the difference between making the cutoff time and exceeding it, but I decide to be conservative and not to push the pace.

I'm expecting Carl to catch up to me with his giant strides, but he never does. Flanked by aspens, I take the jeep road past a spectacular waterfall coming off the mountain to my right. The water cascades hundreds of feet in at least seven stages. It's another place that I regret having to hurry past, but the sight raises my spirits. Like a traveler from an antique land, I enter the aid station armed with the resolve to finish this race, either under 48 hours or over the time limit, but nevertheless I'm going to finish.

Sherman aid station number nine, 70.1-mile point, 9,640 feet. Actually, this aid station should be called Cataract since it is set up at the head of the Cataract Gulch trail, but instead it is named for an abandoned mining town. Judy, Walt, and Helen, all smiles, are here to greet me. What have I done to deserve these people?

"Hey, everybody, how ya doin'?"

"You're doing great, Bob. It's 1:15. You're still ahead of the 48 hour schedule." I'm pleased with this news. I've purposely not been consulting my watch because I feel that I am going as fast as the circumstances permit, and I don't want to beat up on myself if I'm falling behind the cutoff.

"I'm going to take off these fleece pants and change my shirt. I'll need some fresh socks, too, and can you locate the duct tape? I need to put some on my heel." This leads to a comical scene where my crew people hand me several things at once as I am trying to balance on one foot to pull off my pants while at the same time eating my lasagna microwave lunch.

"Hey, wait a minute. Let me sit down and do one thing at a time. Food first."

Helen is wearing gaiters to keep the rocks out of her shoes and leather cyclist half-gloves to protect her hands in case she falls on sharp-edged rocks. She has her backpack on and is ready to pace me.

I'm worried about getting fried by the sun in this next section, so I put on an old white shirt with three-quarter length customized sleeves that I have worn in many ultras. If it becomes too hot, I just unbutton it but it still protects me from sunburn. The next crew access point is a long way from here-twenty-two miles.

"The next time I see you will be in the middle of the night at Cunningham. I'll need to take some more clothes with me now. Can you tie my windbreaker to my vest and somehow fasten my nylon pants onto my vest? I need my lucky Powerbar hat too."

I guess I'm ready. Next aid station: 9.6 miles.

Karl Meltzer pulled ahead of Kirk Apt and Dale Petersen coming over Handies and passed through Sherman at 1:47 a.m., but Kirk was only ten minutes behind him. The climb over Handies took its toll on Dale and he checked into Sherman at 2:23 a.m. Blake Wood was still an hour behind the leader at this point, but had gained 2 1/2 hours on his '97 time. Among the women, Betsy Kalmeyer arrived at Sherman at 3:52 a.m., half an hour ahead of Sue Johnston, who was running without a pacer. Betsy Nye had a rough night and was over an hour behind Sue.

Walking across the road to the trailhead, we receive a small round of applause from the gathered crew members and volunteers.

I respond with a wave, a grin, and a "Thankyouverymuch," in my best Elvis voice.

A decision-making situation immediately presents itself. Other than splashing across, crossing on a large log is the only way to traverse the swift-flowing Cottonwood Creek. Should I try to walk the log or crawl across? Normally, I would walk the log, but at this point in the race I'm not certain of my balance, and I recall what happened the last time I tried to cross a stream on a log. I don't want to pitch headfirst into Cottonwood Creek. I recognize Rock Cogar among some people standing alongside the creek. He and his wife are from Oak Ridge, Tennessee, and are crewing for Leslie Hunt and Kerry Trammell. They all ran the Uwharrie Trail race in February.

"Hi, Bob," Rock greets me. "Some of the runners have been sliding across the log on their butts either straddling it or with both their legs hanging off one side. That way if you do fall off you will land in the creek on your feet."

"Sounds like a plan. The log's too big for me to straddle so I guess I'll do the side saddle slide. Thanks, Rock."

Seating myself on the log with my legs dangling above the rushing water I push myself up from the log with my hands and begin inching across-push up, swing butt, sit down; push up, swing butt, sit down-it's all in the technique-until I've reached the other side and can jump off the log onto the stream bank. Glancing back, I observe Helen stroll nonchalantly across the log like she's out shopping at the mall: makes me feel like a weinie.

Wide and fine, Cataract Gulch trail is popular with day hikers, switchbacking upward through a cathedral of pines with Cataract Creek on our right. Further to our right on the other side of the gulch rise towering granite formations topped with fir trees. Soon the trail straightens out and we reach the first creek crossing. Above us is Cataract Falls and above the falls another creek crossing. In past years a log bridge spanned the creek, but this spring it was swept over the falls. In his long briefing, Charlie warned us that this might be a dangerous place. The powerful current could knock us off our feet and carry us over the 80-foot falls.

When we arrive, Helen forages upstream looking for a good place to cross. It's not as bad as Charlie led us to believe, and she locates a ford. We get our feet wet, but it's gotten to the point where I wonder if something is wrong when my feet are dry. Once we cross the creek, we are confronted by a man and woman walking toward us with two unleashed dogs, one of which rushes at us barking and baring his teeth. I stop so that doggieboy doesn't get the idea that I am a threat to his mommy and daddy, and glare at the people as they walk past us.

Carrying on, we cross the creek a couple of more times until we leave it behind, traverse a rocky area, and climb to the left. Here another runner catches up with us. We exchange "hey, how're ya doins?" This guy has white hair and looks very familiar. He has what sounds to me like a Scottish accent. I know I've met him somewhere before, and it bugs me that I can't pin it down. This is a part of the course where in past years hikers have removed ribbons. Today it isn't overmarked, but ribbons pop up occasionally; it's the only trail in sight, and I'm having no trouble following it. He is quite concerned about staying on the course.

"Have you seen a ribbon lately?" he inquires.

"Ya, we passed one a while back. Don't worry, I've been here before and we're doing fine. Don't I know you?"

"I was lost for two hours coming down Engineers Pass Road. I was with another runner and his pacer took us on the wrong road toward Lake City."

I don't say anything. The briefings and course description all stress the point that you're supposed to go downhill not uphill on Engineers Pass Road and follow the signs to Animas Forks and Silverton, not to Lake City. The guy was probably sleepy at the time. It's easy to let someone else take over and do the thinking in that type of situation.

"Are you from Scotland?" I ask. This is driving me crazy.

"No, I grew up in Ireland." Then it dawns on me.

"You bought a book from me, didn't you?"

"Yes, at the Old Dominion race."

"That's right, I remember you now. Pete, isn't it?"

"No." Mr. Mystery Man keeps falling back then catching up with us like he is into some sort of run/walk routine. Then it dawns on me.

"It's Jim, isn't it."

"Yes, that's right." Jim Magill from California is a Grand Slammer who finished the Old Dominion, Western States, Leadville, and Wasatch Front 100 milers a couple of years ago.

Helen and I break out of the woods and continue through some mushy willows until we reach Cataract Lake. The trail skirts the eastern shore of the lake that sits on top of the continental divide. It's a sunny day in a pretty place and I feel like pausing to sit down, eat something, visit with Helen, and just enjoy the setting, but that scenario will have to wait for another day. We push on past the lake a little higher to the Cataract-Pole Creek Pass, at 12,200 feet, finishing the eighth significant climb.

"What's your favorite movie running scene?" I ask Helen.

"I like the ones in *Last of the Mohicans* where Daniel Day-Lewis runs through the woods. They were filmed in the mountains of western North Carolina," she replies.

"That's a good one. My favorite is in *Out of Africa* where Meryl Streep is bringing supplies to Lord Delamere and the other Brits fighting Germans in East Africa. She's sweating and driving an ox wagon across this shimmering dry lakebed when in the distance she spies a dozen figures trotting toward her. They're Masai warriors wearing these terrific lion's mane headdresses and carrying spears and shields. The camera lingers on them as they approach, then cuts to Streep and the Africans with her, who are all petrified that they are going to be chopped up by these guys. But the Masai just run right past them. It's like they are so absorbed in their own effort, so involved in the purity of their own movement that they can't be bothered to stop and kill Streep and the others. Later in the movie the Robert Redford character says the Masai are the only Africans who aren't interested in becoming westernized. Their own culture provides them with everything they need."

I'm into my movie memory, motoring along, pretending I'm a Masai warrior, not paying much attention to race business, when Helen puts a stop to my daydreaming,

"Turn right here, Bob," she calls out.

After thirty-plus hours, my concentration is wavering. Without Helen I would have run right past the well-marked turn. This is the reason having a companion runner at this stage of the race is important. It's unethical for pacers to run ahead at aid stations and fill their runners' bottles so they don't have to stop or for pacers to carry extra water bottles for tired runners. But it's okay for pacers to point runners in the right direction. Their job is to keep runners safe and on course.

The flags lead us to the next section of the course, which is a downhill, cross country trek through mucky willows, across streams and swampy meadows that brings us to the Colorado Trail, which is also the Continental Divide Trail at this point. Lo and behold, it's runnable. Kirk Apt told me that this is a good place to gain some time if I'm battling the cutoffs, so I break into my enhanced high altitude shuffle. This pace is designed to eat up the miles without exhausting me. Ironically, this is where Kirk Apt's quads gave up earlier today and he began to fall behind the leaders. Helen has been following quietly, so I shout back to her.

"This is easy terrain. I'm trying to move faster."

"I noticed. No problem, you're doing fine."

I'm in good spirits and have a decent energy level although I'm not eating as many GUs, gels, and Powerbites as I was yesterday. This is probably a mistake.

We're jamming through a valley with spectacular 13.000-foot snowcapped ridges on both sides. It's called the La Garita Stock Driveway and is one of my favorite parts of the Hardrock course because I can take my eyes off the trail and enjoy the scenery while moving at a respectable pace. "*La Garita*" means "lookout" and refers to the Ute Indians' use of the surrounding peaks as vantage points to keep track of the Spanish explorers who crossed the San Juans on their way west. With so much water and grazing area for their horses, plus elk to hunt, this must have been a favorite summer campground for the Ute. During the mining heyday, ranchers drove herds of sheep and cattle through here with the idea of selling them in the mining settlements in the vicinity of Handies, Sunshine, and Redcloud Peaks.

From time to time I spy two runners ahead of us. We catch up with one of them at a willow bog and it turns out to be Harry Smith.

"Hi, Harry. It's me again. Didn't we run together for a while last night?" At this point my short term memory isn't too sharp. It takes an effort to concentrate my attention on anything beyond forward motion.

"Yes, Bob, that was on Camp Bird Road coming down into Ouray."

"You look like you're moving pretty well. We'll just stay behind and let you take the lead."

Helen and I maintain a steady pace. From time to time we catch up to Harry; then he speeds up and puts some distance between us. At the briefing Charlie warned us about possible difficulties at two Pole Creek crossings. Arriving at the first one, we find the water moving quickly, but it doesn't look deep so we splash across. Helen goes ahead to reconnoiter the second one. It looks worse, with a lot of water surging through the narrow creek bed.

"I can't find any better place to cross than here, Bob," Helen reports, and we side step our way across without incident.

We have the next aid station in sight ahead of us and to our left near a grove of trees and we've run down Harry again. Horses are tethered next to some tents, and people are waving at us. We wave back, but apparently they aren't greeting us. Instead, they are pointing to their left where another group of people is standing. That must be Pole Creek aid station, number ten at the 80-mile point, elevation: 11,260 feet.

The aid station volunteers are all excited when we arrive.

"We've got a helicopter coming in to evacuate one of the runners in a few minutes. What can we do for you?" says the lady at the food shelter.

"What's wrong with him? Do you have any potato soup?" I ask.

"We can't tell you. Yes, we have," she says.

"Why can't you tell us? Can I have a banana?" I ask.

"We just can't. Yes," she replies. My curiosity is aroused by this woman's refusal to divulge important information. Maybe I can bamboozle her into telling me by being nice, by playing the good cop.

"Thanks a lot for the soup. It tastes really good." Actually, it's just instant potatoes poured into warm water and stirred. It needs salt.

"Where are you from?" I inquire.

"Durango," she responds.

"Oh, that's a pretty town." She brightens up. I've hooked her.

"We like to think so," she says proudly.

"Does the runner have a broken leg? Why can't he just walk to the next aid station?" I ask.

"I can't tell you anything," she says. A tough nut to crack. She isn't falling for any of my tricks. After all this hearty exercise above the tree line, I have developed a small cough. A young fellow with a stethoscope hanging from his neck appears in front of me.

"Mind if I check your lungs?" he asks. "I'm trying to get all the experience I can with you runners."

"Sure, why not." I like to help out the medical community whenever I can. This is probably the EMT who made the decision to call in the helicopter. Since I'm getting nowhere with Ms. Potato Soup maybe I can get the story out of him. I adopt a man-to-man conspiratorial tone.

"Hey, what's going on with the medivac?" I ask using my extensive military vocabulary. "Are you going to have to carry him to the chopper?"

"No, he can walk." Success. A vital fact has been established. It's not a broken leg. What could it be? Think. It must be something life threatening if they are going to all the expense of flying him out of here. If it's something ordinary like dehydration the next aid station is only five miles away. He can drink his fill then walk out. The only other helicopter evacuation I can recall during a 100-mile trail race was one year at Leadville when a lady got sick at the top of Hope Pass and had to be flown out. Landing a small helicopter at 12,000 feet on Hope Pass was dangerous, and the race organizers were not pleased. Wait a minute, I've got it.

"Does he have cerebral edema?" I ask.

"Nope," he replies.

"Pulmonary edema?" I try again. He's finished listening to my lungs wheeze.

"Nope. You sound all right." At least I'm not a candidate for evacuation. Before I can think of any more life threatening injuries one of the volunteers yells, 'Here comes Carolyn."

Must be Carolyn Erdman catching up with me.

Helen is at my side; "Time to go, Bob."

"Ya, you're right; 104 checking out."

"Keep to the left of a muddy place in the trail," one of the volunteers shouts after us. "It's marked with a stick."

As we depart the aid station the helicopter appears from the southeast. The sound made by the blades whirling around is familiar to me from the years I've spent at Fort Bragg. Watching it land I ask Helen, "Did anyone tell you what his trouble is?"

"Yes, he had blood in his urine."

"Blood in his urine. Is that all? They've gone to all the trouble of bringing in a helicopter to evacuate someone with blood in his urine? That doesn't make any sense." I'm ranting. "Normally, if a runner has blood in his urine it means he's dehydrated and the walls of his bladder have collapsed and are rubbing together. The rubbing irritates the lining of the bladder and produces blood that is peed out. All you have to do is re-hydrate and your problem is solved. I've seen it more than once in these races."

"I dunno. Maybe they are being extra careful and don't want another Joel Zucker situation," Helen says.

At the front of the race, Karl Meltzer arrives at Pole Creek at 5:27 a.m., twenty miles and thirteen hours ahead of me. Kirk Apt is twenty-five minutes behind Karl, and Randy Isler is twelve minutes behind Kirk. Blake Wood lost some time in the dark due to flashlight problems. He is fifty minutes behind Karl, but after the sun comes up he feels like a new man and begins running hard. Among the women, Betsy Kalmeyer pulls in to the aid station at 7:24 a.m. She is followed by Sue Johnston at 7:52. Betsy Nye arrives one hour and 18 minutes after Sue.

While Helen and I were at Pole Creek, a runner passed through without stopping.

"Did you see that guy run right through the aid station?" I ask her. "I'll bet he was the one we saw a couple of times in front of us who disappeared. We never passed him so the only way we could get in front of him is if he was lost. I think it was Todd Burgess."

How do I know that? I must have overheard someone at the Sherman aid station mention Todd. Strange how the mind works in these situations. In some ways I'm hyper alert, in others I'm completely useless.

The last twenty miles of any hundred-mile race are always crucial for me. This is where I invariably run out of gas, so I have learned to stop and eat something at every aid station, even if it's just a few cookies and a cup of Coke two miles from the finish line. If I fail to ingest sugar at the end of a race, I'm liable to collapse from hypoglycemia. The same is true for salt. I need to keep my electrolytes balanced so my system will digest the food I take in.

We're back on the Continental Divide Trail still following the La Garita Stock Drive. It's 5.5 miles to the next aid station. Remembering the volunteer's caution about the muddy spot on the trail I tell Helen, "You know, last year I was on a training run on this trail. When I came to this one muddy place I tried to jump across but didn't quite make it, landed in the mud with one foot and sunk in up to my knee. My other foot landed on firm ground and I managed to pull my muddy leg out without losing my shoe, but that leg didn't touch the bottom of that mudhole. I'll bet that's the place they are talking about."

"Let's watch for the stick in the mud up ahead," Helen says.

"Did I ever tell you about the planeload of Pepsi Cola that was being flown from South Africa to the Congo?" I inquire.

"No, you didn't," Helen responds.

"Well, the plane crashed in the Congo near a village full of cannibals. A search plane was sent from Johannesburg to look for the downed aircraft and find out what happened to the crew. They spotted the wreckage and landed near the village, but when they reached the plane there was no sign of the crew. Returning to the village they asked the chief if he knew what happened to the crew.

"He said, 'We're cannibals. We ate them.'

"Appalled, the search team leader said, 'You mean you ate their arms?'

"The chief replied, 'Yes, indeed, and we washed them down with Pepsi Cola.'

"The search team leader's face paled.

"He asked, 'And you ate their legs?'

"The smiling chief said, 'Yes, indeed, and we washed them down with Pepsi Cola.'

"The search team leader really looked ill now. He gulped a couple of times then said, 'And what about their... you know... their things?'

"The chief shook his finger in the white man's face. 'No, no,' he said. 'Things go better with Coke.'"

"Ha, ha, ha. That's a good one, Bob," Helen chortles. "Did you hear about the guy who was driving down the Los Angeles freeway in a convertible with two penguins sitting in the back seat?" Helen inquires.

"No, I haven't. Is this a true story?" I ask.

"Why, of course it is, Bob. All my stories are true. Anyway, a California highway patrolman on a motorcycle roars out of his hiding place and pulls the convertible over. The cop is furious. 'What are you doing with two penguins in the back seat of your convertible?' he demands. 'Take these birds to the zoo at once.' So the guy drives off.

"The next day the same thing happens but this time the penguins are wearing sunglasses. The motorcycle cop stops the convertible and is all ticked off. 'I thought I told you to take these penguins to the zoo,' he shouts. 'I did,' the driver replies. 'Today we're going to the beach.'"

"Good one, Helen. I'm going to have to remember that one."

We come to the mudhole the volunteer mentioned.

"Yup, that's the place. Avoid it or you'll be sorry," I observe.

We're passing through a willow swamp area. The so-called "trail" here is all mud and water. I'm bouncing back and forth from one side of the "trail" to the other side trying to stay out of the mud with little success. If we're not in a swamp then we're splashing through a stream. It's impossible to tell if this is just one stream-the West Fork of Pole Creek-that is meandering or if these are permanent tributary streams or just new streams created by snowmelt, but I'm getting really fed up with all the water.

"Helen, this race is all about two things-wet feet," I yell.

"Lots of water up here, Bob," Helen says agreeably.

"That was a joke. Did you get it?" I ask.

"Ya, Bob. I got it," she replies.

My mouth won't stay shut. Must be something I ate at the last aid station.

"You know, Helen, one plus this year is that there are fewer elk turds mixed in with the mud. In past years you could smell a runner coming before you could see him. This year the stink isn't so bad."

"That's interesting, Bob. I'm glad I picked a low elk turd year."

The wind is in our faces and it's getting dark. I start looking for someplace to change into warmer clothes. On the far side of the next stream crossing we find shelter in the lee of a cliff.

"Hey, Helen, let's stop here and put on some more clothes. Do you have a jacket you can put on? It's going to get cold now with the sun going down."

"Bob, I'm fully prepared for everything."

I'm pulling on my nylon running pants and windbreaker, but I'm going to need warmer headgear than my Powerbar cap.

"Great, do you have an extra knit hat? Something I can pull over my ears?"

"Sure, here you go." She hands me a kind of skullcap-red with other colors mixed in-that I immediately fall in love with.

"Okay, let's get moving." I've been expecting Carolyn Erdman to catch up with us, but there's no sign of her.

We continue on an easy ascent and reach the top of Maggie-Pole Pass at 12,530 feet, climb number nine. Still some snow up here. The trail swings off to the right. Soon the next aid station on Maggie Gulch Road comes into view, far below us. The trail switchbacks on the long downhill until we reach the road. I'm feeling a little down, more desperate than victorious, as we turn left and jog into the penultimate aid station in the race, number eleven at the 85.2 mile point, Maggie Gulch, at 11,640 feet.

143

Lisa Richardson, her Australian-born husband, Darin, and their two labs, one yellow and one black, are taking care of runners here. Being greeted by Lisa's hundred-watt personality brightens my outlook. I can't afford to spend a lot of time here, but I want to eat something because I know I'll need every speck of energy I can muster for the next climb.

"Hey, Lisa, number 104 and pacer checking in. How ya doin? Got any soup for us?"

"Yes, the specialty of the house is mixed chicken noodle and potato. I'm sorry. With so many runners I don't know your name."

"It's Bob from North Carolina. You've got some friendly dogs here. My yellow lab, Sandy Boeder, died last year. He was fourteen."

"That's old for one of these large dogs. Here's your soup. And a spoon to eat it with."

The dogs are rushing back and forth eager to go with us, but Lisa calls them back.

Departing the aid station I shout, "104 and pacer checking out; I'll see you at the finish line."

It's 9:00 p.m. I've no idea what the cutoff time is at this aid station. I've been on my feet for 39 hours. Lisa is a beautiful young blond woman with an expressive face. When I tell her I'll see her at the finish line she doesn't respond with her usual dazzling smile. The look she gives me communicates the thought, "You poor bastard, you'll never make it."

Nearly fourteen hours previously, at 7:19 a.m., Karl Meltzer pulled into Maggie Gulch. He spent eight minutes at the aid station. When he left at 7:27, Blake Wood was ten minutes behind him. Blake ran the 5.5 miles from Pole Creek to Maggie Gulch in one hour and ten minutes, overtaking Kirk Apt and Randy Isler along the way. All of a sudden he's in second place. Phenomenal for someone who was in eighth place at Sherman, fifteen miles back. Betsy reaches Maggie Gulch at 9:00 a.m. and only stays a few minutes. Sue

Johnston is 28 minutes behind her and running strongly. Next aid station: 6.9 miles.

Exiting from the Maggie Gulch aid station, we scramble over a culvert in order to cross the inevitable stream and gain the Martha Mine Road. Following the switchbacking road past an abandoned caterpillar tractor, we reach a place where the course markers take us sharply to the right, off the road and up onto a grassy slope. Here we connect with Crystal Lake trail, which we follow up the side of a steep gully. From this point the course markers take us straight up the side of Buffalo Boy Ridge which tops out at 13,000 feet. Straight up. The aid station is at 11,640 feet. For me this is where the true suffering begins. No more jokes. No more ranting. Like the song says, "Everybody hurts, hold on, hold on." I'm glad it's dark so Helen can't see what this is costing me.

Most of the time I'm on all fours. Gasping. Ascend fifteen to twenty feet then stop when I get to a small flat place on the hillside where I can rest on one knee. A week ago I brought Helen and John out here and we climbed this slope. I told Helen to take a good look around and remember the landmarks because come race day I would depend on her to take me up this mountain in the dark. This is where I need her.

I'm carrying a flashlight, but my head is down close to the ground. Helen has a strong light and it's up to her to pick out the next flag marker. The wind moans like a ghost song. I'm so grateful that she is with me, but that feeling doesn't come out in the desperate tone of my voice.

"Where's the next marker? Can you see it? Shine your light on it so I can see it."

The flags are few and far between. Some of them are facing away from us so they don't reflect when Helen shines her light in their direction. I'm concentrating all of my energy on each uphill scramble. Fifteen feet and stop. In the months before he died, my dog, Sandy, would often collapse during his nightly walk. His legs would just crumble under him and he would lie there in the street panting. Fifteen feet and collapse. I would pet Sandy, scratch his ears, encourage him, and eventually he would gather himself, struggle to his feet, and take a few more steps. That's the way I feel now. Like some old yellow dog on his last legs being led to his final bowl of Friskies.

Ahead of us from time to time we can see two points of light moving up the mountain. I assume that Jim Magill and Harry Smith have teamed up. Another beam of light flickers to our left and above us indicating a runner is off the course. Occasionally, we can hear some yelling from that direction, but it's too distant to make out what is being said. It must be Todd Burgess. I assume that if we can see his light, he can see ours. It must be obvious to him that he has lost the course markers, and, therefore, he should come in our direction. If he is thinking clearly.

Our targets are two large rock outcrops. We stay to the left of the first one. The second one is frightening. Until now Helen and I have been climbing side by side. Conversation has been held to the minimum. I'm not wasting my breath on small talk. Below the second outcrop Helen speaks up.

"I'll take the lead, Bob. Just follow me and put your feet where I put mine." Fine with me. Crystal Lake lies 500 feet down a steep, snow-covered slope to my right. I want to keep my body out of the icy lake water, so I step where Helen steps and up we go. It's one of those places like the final approach to the Virginius Pass aid station, where stopping for a breather is not an option. You either do this in one quick burst of energy or you wind up on your belly sliding backwards to God only knows where.

We make it to the top of the outcrop and our momentum keeps us going. The trail angles left up here through a grassy area. In 1996, this is where I came upon Kawika Spaulding enjoying himself smoking a cigarette.

One final climb lies between us and the top of the ridge. The slope is steep and snow covered. Footsteps have been kicked in the frozen snow by previous runners. Again, all we have to do is keep moving our feet as fast as we can and we should have no trouble with this icy foot ladder. Helen leads the way. I wait until she is half way up then follow. The slope is all ice. My feet slip a couple of times, but I make it to the summit of Buffalo Boy Ridge safely. Climb number ten: 13,060 feet.

The flags lead us along a grassy mesa. Off to the right on the edge of the ridge with a terrific view of endless mountaintops is Bob Green's marble grave marker. Course markers bring us to the Buffalo Boy mine jeep road which we follow down past the remains of the mine and tram shed. The tram carried ore from the mine down to the mill on Cunningham Gulch Road, our destination tonight. I allow myself a moment of triumph when the tram shed looms in the darkness. It's around 11:00; I should be able to reach the final aid station in time to make a dash for the finish, but my celebration is short lived.

My race strategy called for me to move quickly on the downhill road sections of the course, but once again I fail. This time a rocky road is to blame. The road up here near the mine is like an uneven stream bed composed of rocks of varying sizes. Snowmelt has eroded gullies in the road, so we have to keep switching sides to find a section that is even walkable. My feet are sore and blistered and I can hardly stand up in some places, much less run. I did not train on this section of the course this year, but I've been up here several times in past years, and it never dawned on me that this would be the slowest part of the entire course for me.

"Helen, I can't go any faster. What are we going to do?" I beg plaintively.

"Just hang in there, Bob. These rocks can't last forever."

She's right, but even when we reach a gravel road the smaller rocks are still killing me. I can't even shuffle. Jetman, where are you when I need you? All I can do is walk. Appropriately, this road separates Rocky Gulch from Stony Gulch.

The descent becomes a long trudge down a rough road on a dark and cheerless night. This must be the way it feels to be an auk-flightless, on the verge of extinction. Defeated, I have nothing to say to Helen. Sensing my mood, she keeps quiet. Occasionally through the trees downhill to my right we can see the lights of vehicles on Cunningham Gulch Road. They seem closer than they actually are. We splash through several streams. The cold water soothes my tender feet so I've stopped complaining about being wet.

I'm concentrating on turning right when we reach Stony Pass Road, not left. Taking a left sends us in the direction of Creede, Colorado, which is not part of the plan. Eventually, we reach the intersection I think I have been looking for. I turn to the right.

Helen says, "Wait a minute, Bob. This is where we turn left."

"No, no," I argue. "I've been looking for this intersection for an hour. We've got to turn right to get to Cunningham Gulch Road."

"But, this is Cunningham Gulch Road, Bob. Look at the sign over there. The aid station is this way, to the left."

I walk over to the sign at the corner of the road. She's correct. Silverton to the right. How did I miss the turn onto Stony Pass Road? I have no idea. I didn't really miss it. I took it, but I had no idea what I was doing. I guess I was feeling so sorry for myself that I just zoned out, went on cruise control.

It's a mile and a half to the aid station. A car driven by a woman passes us heading toward town.

"Way to go," she yells out the window. "Keep it up."

What the hell do you know, I think to myself. She's probably crewing for some guy who will finish in under 48 hours. Bully for him. That isn't going to be one of my options. I haven't looked at my watch recently, but it seems like we've been walking forever. Up ahead someone is coming toward us carrying a flashlight.

We meet and whoever it is turns around to join us. I hope it isn't some yeh-rah-rah type who is going to give me a pep talk. I've been going over my options in my mind-quit or hang in there for an unofficial finish-and I've just about decided to drop out. I've lost my motivation. There seems to be no point in carrying on.

"Hello, are you both runners?" flashlightman speaks.

After a pause Helen answers for me. "No, I'm a pacer and he's the runner." She's a woman. Let her do the talking.

"I'm Aaron," he introduces himself. "Like in the Bible. What's your name?" Who cares? Why doesn't this guy shut up? Another pause.

"I'm Helen." I remain silent.

"What's your name?" he asks. Persistent fellow. What is this? Twenty questions? I suppose I've got to say something.

"I'm Bob. B-O-B. It's spelled the same backwards and forwards." No last name. I'm being sarcastic, trying to make Aaron angry so he'll go away, but instead he laughs.

"Well B-O-B it's 1:00 in the morning. The aid station closes at 1:30 so you still have time to beat the cutoff. Is anyone meeting you?"

Crap. To have a chance at finishing under 48 hours I had to get to Cunningham by midnight. That would give me six hours to do the final 9.6 miles. Once Joel made it in five hours, but he had to run like a madman. With my tender feet and my bad attitude that's not going to happen tonight.

"Ya, our crew is there to meet us," I reply warming up a little. "Where are you from?"

"Los Alamos," he replies. "Most of the volunteers at Cunningham work at the national lab there."

"Oh, ya. Los Alamos is a real trail runner hotbed-Charlie and Blake and all those guys live there. Do you know Aaron Goldman?" I ask rather stupidly.

"Yes, that's me. I'm Aaron Goldman." Boy, do I feel dumb. How many Aarons from Los Alamos can there be?

"In 1994 at the Leadville 100 I was right behind you when you stepped in a pothole and broke your ankle," I say excitedly. "I couldn't believe they didn't repair the street before the race. It wasn't more than 100 yards from the start."

"You must be Bob Boeder. You wrote about me in your book." This is like old home week. This encounter with

Aaron Goldman brightens my outlook as the lights of the aid station come into view. Cunningham aid station number twelve; 92.1 mile point: 10,380 feet.

A certain amount of confusion reigns as we turn right off Cunningham Gulch Road and enter the aid station area. People descend on us in the dark and I can't tell who they are.

Someone yells, "It's 1:20. He should check in then check out right away." This would insure that I beat the 1:30 cutoff time.

Someone else replies, "No, let's not do that." At this point I'm really not interested in proceeding so I don't care about the cutoff time.

Another person grabs my arm and says urgently, "What can I get you?" I hate it when aid station people get all hyper and try to drag me to the food table.

Shaking off his grip I respond, "Thanks, we've got a crew."

John appears out of the darkness. He's dressed for cold weather in a warm jacket, gloves and a balaclava. "Bob, I'm ready to spend three more nights with you if that's what it takes to finish."

Wow. "Thanks, John." That's dedication. He's prepared to help me. I'm reluctant to tell him the bad news. Walt and Judy are waiting at the lighted area where vehicles are parked. A gas stove with some pots on it is perched on the tailgate of a pickup truck. Shedding my jacket and my vest, I slump into a folding chair. A sigh of exhaustion escapes into the cold night air.

Walt greets me, but his customary cheerfulness is subdued probably because of my haggard appearance. "Nice going, Bob. You got here before the cutoff. What's your plan?"

"You mean, am I going on or am I going to stop here? I'm leaning toward calling it a night."

"Well, at least you've set a new personal PR on this course."

I like this idea. At least something is salvaged from my effort. Ninety-two miles beats my previous best of 56 last year. I'm not in a real big decision-making mood at this point. One of the volunteers hands me a cup of chicken noodle soup and asks, "Are you going on?"

"I don't know. I really don't feel like it, but I'm undecided." Checking out my body nothing is broken or hurting badly so there is no outstanding physical reason for not continuing. Basically, my feet hurt, I'm worn out, and I lack resolve.

Looking for sympathy, I tell Walt, "I've got the same problem you had at Western States-bad feet." He's too much of a friend to remind me that even though his feet were much worse off than mine are now he still finished the race.

Aaron Goldman speaks to me, "Bob, take as long as you like to make your decision." He's the race official in charge of this aid station. That means he is waiving the 1:30 cutoff for me. I'm struck by this gesture of kindness. As an ultrarunner himself, Aaron has been where I am now and he understands my situation. He wants me to finish, but he's not in my face forcing anything on me.

The volunteers have drifted off to talk among themselves. I'm sitting in my chair wrapped in my blanket, sipping on my cup of soup, and watching my crew people. One of them is staring back at me. Maybe glaring is a better word for it. It's Judy. She hasn't said anything, but her face says a lot. She is a strong person. I respect her. She looks ticked off. At me. I make a feeble attempt at charming her into joining me on the dropout wagon.

"I've thought of a dropping out speech," I inform her.

"What is it?" she replies.

"I gave this race everything I had, but it wasn't enough."

Judy isn't impressed. She and the others have been out here for two days and two nights. They're not giving up. It's decision time. If I drop out the ride back to town is going to be grim. I don't care about myself at this point. If it was just me I would hang it up, but these people have supported me so loyally that I can't let them down.

"Okay, I'll continue. I need my last microwave meal and my gore-tex jacket and pants."

"All right. Way to go." Smiles all around. My last microwave supper is chicken with noodles.

Blake Wood came through Cunningham at 7:22 a.m. and paused for only a few minutes to pick up his pacer, Igor, before leaving. He was concerned about Randy Isler, trailing Blake by 27 minutes, but known for his late race surge. Hans Put was ten minutes behind Randy. When Karl Meltzer pulled into Cunningham at 8:08 a.m. he dropped out of the race. His quads were shot. Betsy Kalmeyer arrived at 9:07 and spent ten minutes fueling up. Picking up Dick Curtis to pace her, she shot out of the aid station on a mission-to finish in under 32 hours. Sue Johnston was maintaining her pace 27 minutes behind Betsy, the same gap separating Blake and Randy.

As John and I leave the aid station, everyone applauds and cheers. I shout "Viva, Viva" in reply. That's what the Cubans taught South Africans to say when they were fighting for their independence against the white minority government. It's 1:40 a.m. and 9.6 miles to the finish.

Cunningham Creek always has a strong current here, so I'm apprehensive about this crossing, but strangely the water level has gone way down and we have no trouble walking across. John has forgotten something so he dashes back to the aid station while I stride uphill at an angle through skunk cabbage to the Dives Creek ford. Once across I pick up the Shenandoah Mine trail and John rejoins me as we commence our long trek up into Dives Basin. It's a 2 1/2 mile climb with an elevation gain of 2,600 feet to the top. On a normal day it takes me an hour and a half to do this climb. The course is so overgrown with willow bushes that occasionally the trail just disappears and we have to push through the bushes, hope we haven't missed any turns, and look for flags reflecting our flashlight beams up ahead.

In previous 100-mile races I have always experienced aching in the upper part of my back which I assumed was lung soreness due to heavy breathing over an extended time. Up until now the great thing about this race has been the absence of lung ache, but that comes to a screeching halt as we tackle this ascent. Along with the soreness comes an occasional cough and spitting up of phlegm. Adding this discomfort to my general exhaustion reduces my pace to something less than a crawl-close to a creep. The words *glacial* and *snail* come to mind. I take ten slow steps then I have to pause to catch my breath. As we ascend, it gets worse. I'm in a place beyond endurance-the Antarctic of the soul.

Momentarily I consider quitting and returning to the aid station, but I'm so far up the trail I might as well finish the climb. Searching for relief I put my hands on my waist and stick out my chest. Breathing is less uncomfortable this way. Apparently, it gives my lungs more room to expand, but I still have to stop every thirty feet. At this rate it will take us the three nights John promised to spend with me to get to the top of this mountain.

In the past the thought of spending a second night on the trail scared me. Well, here I am in the middle of it and the words that come to mind are *drip, ooze, inch*. It's the slowest I have ever moved in my trail running life.

I've been using the same Garrity Life Lite all evening. It has served me well, but now the bulb dims. No matter. I pull out my Princeton Tec light with its powerful beam, but twenty seconds later it winks out. Oops. All of a sudden I'm down to one light, my backup Garrity Life Lite. At the same time as I am fumbling around with my flashlights John's headlamp goes out.

"What's going on?" I ask John. "Do you have any more lights?"

"I've got backup batteries for my headlamp, and if all else fails I've got a penlight." In a matter of moments our flashlight supply has been cut in half from six to three.

John says, "This is like the movie *The Outlaw Josey Wales,* where Clint Eastwood keeps pulling out revolvers to shoot the bad guys, only we're doing it with flashlights." I can't think of any Josey Wales movie quotes to respond to John, so I keep quiet for a change.

Dives Basin is off the cliff to our left. Visible in daylight are the remains of the Shenandoah Mine and the wreckage of a bulldozer that was driven off the edge of a large pile of mine tailings forty years ago. We are in total darkness. The main sensation is the sound of Dives Creek as it cascades into Cunningham Gulch. I have the same fear of falling off the trail into the basin as I had last night on Bear Creek Trail, but tonight I'm leaning to my right. Since I can't visually orient myself to anything, it is difficult to tell if we are making progress. As the climb drags on I get the distinct impression that we have been here before.

"Hey, John, didn't we just go up this trail? It seems that we are going around in circles."

"Not that I know of, Bob."

"Look, we just took this right turn and we're doing it again. What the hell is going on?" I'm getting irritated. John's the pacer. It's his job to keep us on the course.

"We're supposed to go straight up the mountain at some point, but it's not happening. I just climbed over these rocks and now I'm doing it again over the same damn rocks."

"Take it easy, Bob. We'll get there." My situation keeps deteriorating. This is strictly a survival trip now. I must keep moving in order to stay alive. At least that's what I'm thinking.

Finally, the course markers take off straight up the hill.

"Okay, Bob. Here's where we start our climb."

"What the hell do you think we've been doing?" Bad Bob is emerging. This is the ornery fellow you don't want to be around. Actually, feeling mean has positive results in that it makes me combative. All I have to fight is this hill, so my energy is directed toward defeating the hill by climbing to the top.

My lungs are still killing me and I'm still stopping every fifteen feet to gasp for air. John is having trouble picking out the flags up ahead of us.

"Where's the next one, John?"

"I'm not sure. I thought I saw a reflection above us, but I've lost it."

"That's not good enough." To his everlasting credit John, does not strangle me. He perseveres, finds the next flag, and we keep climbing. I can see the outline of the top of the ridge against the sky. Our next challenge is to find Little Giant Pass in the dark.

"That's the pass over there to the right, isn't it, John?" I'm positive we are going in the wrong direction.

"No, it's straight ahead of us."

"But don't you see that well-defined notch in the ridge over there? That's the pass." Nothing like a little argument at four in the morning.

"We're following the flags, Bob. See, there's the pass." The sky is brightening . By golly, he's right. We're at 13,000 feet, Dives-Little Giant Pass, number 11, the top of the final climb.

"Hey, this is it. Nice going, John. Sorry I got on your case back there."

"That's all right. Since I'm in the Army I'm used to being yelled at. Turn around and enjoy the view." Clouds have formed in the basins and gulches below us. Snowy mountain peaks and high ridges poke through the clouds. It's a breathtaking scene.

At the pass, the snow-covered trail follows the side of a cliff leading to Little Giant saddle. To my right a steep grassy slope ends at the top of a sheer cliff that plummets hundreds of feet into a rocky basin. A misstep on the icy surface could be fatal. Footsteps of previous runners have sunk deep into the snowbank that has melted since last weekend when John, Helen, and I were up here. Tonight we cross the snow bridge quickly.

During my previous visits to the snow traverse on training runs, acrophobia has gotten to me, but darkness makes the situation less scary. My stomach doesn't flutter and I actually enjoy being on the wide saddle west of the pass. It's like strolling across a grassy lawn in the sky. Basins open up on opposing sides of the saddle, their floors 1,000 feet below us, but since I'm not close to the edge, I don't feel uneasy. We're aiming for a trail that peels off the saddle to the left that will take us down the northwest side of Little Giant Basin, the start of a 3,000 foot descent to Arrastra Creek. The footing on this trail is terrible-slippery, steep, and rocky, with a long dropoff on our left into the basin where darkness hides some tailings piles and ruined mine buildings. The earth beneath us is full of tunnels from dozens of mines that were worked year round by the hardrock miners.

The trail is so bad I'm not certain that it is the right one, but nothing above or below looks any better, so we carry on.

"We're supposed to pick up a road pretty soon," I inform John. "The going should get easier as we descend."

"Look at that," John points to the side of the trail. "Why would anybody do that here?" On a flat rock right next to the trail someone has deposited a neat pile of turds. It's not the work of an animal because human turds look different, and some soiled butt wipe lies nearby.

"I guess he wanted to mark the spot," I comment. "Probably was too tired to climb up or down to drop his load, but at least he could have waited until he got to the road. Pretty disgusting."

Lower down, the trail is overgrown by willows, but we finally connect with the Little Giant jeep road. This is all downhill. John forages ahead. All I can do is hobble.

"I hope I can get to the finish in under 49 hours," I call out to John. "That will at least be respectable. Last year two guys finished in over 51 hours. I'd just as soon leave them at the bottom of the Hardrock finishers list."

It's light enough to turn off our flashlights. On our left we pass the ruins of Big Giant Mine with what look like boardwalks hanging off some cliffs. Entering the timber, we pass the remains of tram towers before joining Arrastra Gulch road. The first two years that the race was held, the course was mostly road from here to the finish in Memorial Park. In 1994, the finish was moved to the ski hut; the course was transferred from roads to trails and became a lot more difficult.

Looking at my watch I inform John, "It's six o'clock. The race is over. I'll have to settle for an asterisk."

A parked RV comes into view as a long-eared dog that looks like a cross between a beagle and a bloodhound jogs up the road to meet us. Mr. Long Ears has a mixed breed buddy who joins him and gives John and me a smellover. I'll bet I'm exuding an exciting aroma at this stage of the race. The dogs bark a couple of times to signal their boss in the RV that they're on the job and then we leave them behind.

Arrastra Creek looms ahead of us. I'm leery of the volume of water in this stream, but it's not as deep as I feared. On the other side we follow a pipeline that parallels the creek for a while. From time to time through the trees we glimpse Highway 110, the gravel road to Silverton. Passing a white house on our right we join a trail which follows a bench in a southwesterly direction above the Animas River. Jim Benike told me it took him 50 minutes to run from the white house to the finish line during a training run. Checking my watch, it's nearly 7:00 am. Guess I won't make it in under 49 hours.

"John, I'm absolutely determined to finish in under 50 hours," I call out.

The terrain we're encountering is the muckiest of the entire race. Sloppy, muddy, overgrown by willows. We pass several beaver dams and slosh through streams slicing across the trail. Water is everywhere. Is this a new section of the course? I don't remember any of this from the start of the race last year. Just like that sadist Charlie Thorn to add new trail and not tell anyone. From time to time I can see buildings through the trees to my right signaling our arrival on the northeast edge of Silverton. Hillside Cemetery should be somewhere over there across the Animas River.

While I'm moaning and groaning, we come upon the prettiest sight of the entire two days in the wilderness. The sun is shining brightly, and we're in mixed aspen and fir forest when we arrive at a small pond. The surface of the pond is absolutely still and mirrors its surroundings perfectly. John and I pause for a moment. A feeling of serenity envelops me. Looking at the pond then looking at the woods, I can't tell which is reality and which is the reflection. The soreness of my feet breaks my reverie and we move on.

"John, we're supposed to intersect the Silverton ski area, where we angle downhill to the right. I don't know why it's taking so long to get there."

"Shouldn't be too much farther," John replies. Catching occasional glimpses of the town on our right, I feel we're making hardly any progress.

Arriving at one more stream rushing down the side of the hill to the Animas River, I wonder if this will be the final one. It looks dangerous-not wide, but deep with a fast current. A wooden bridge sits uselessly on our side of the creek, as if someone was going to push it across the stream but forgot. Or maybe the stream changed course and the bridge was left high and dry. Still in front of me, John kicks some boulders into the water and one of them lodges against other rocks giving us a stepping stone in the middle of the stream. John goes first. Following him, I reach across the creek with my right hand to grab a tree trunk to pull myself to the other side. A small branch has been snapped off, probably by previous runners, leaving a sharp-edged piece protruding from the trunk right where I place my hand. It feels like a nail has been driven into my hand. It takes a few moments to gently disengage my hand from the tree. Blood pours from the ugly gash.

"Hey, John. Stop for a minute." John trots back to where I am.

"What's up?" he asks.

"I cut my hand. I need you to untie the red bandana around my neck to use as a bandage."

"It doesn't look too bad," John says.

"What do you mean? It's in a bad place between my thumb and forefinger. It's going to need stitches."

"I don't think so." John looks at me like I'm some kind of wimp for wanting my hand sewn up.

"Are you a qualified surgeon?" I inquire. That should shut him up.

"Yes, I am," he replies. Then, after a pause, "Just joking."

Finally we arrive at the ski area turnoff. Limping down the rough, rocky hillside past the former finish line in the ski area parking lot, we cross the Animas River on the 14th street bridge, continue past the red stone City Hall on our left, cross Greene Street, and take the next left on Reese Street. This is the home stretch.

"I guess we can run it in," I tell John.

Breaking into a trot, I feel a surge of adrenaline. Every hormone in my body leaps to attention. My feet don't hurt any more. A plan for what to do when I reach the Hardrock pops into my head. I see Darin and Lisa Richardson in their driveway unloading aid station supplies from their vehicle.

"Hey Lisa," I yell. "I told you I'd see you in Silverton." She gives me a wave and a tired smile.

There's the school up ahead on the corner. That's funny. There's no finish banner, no clock. Some people applaud as we run by. There's the Hardrock in front of the school just where we left it two days ago. Walt, Judy, and Helen along with some other people I don't recognize are standing in the street yelling at me and clapping. No race officials in sight.

I run up to the Hardrock and kiss it. My plan is to climb up and stand on top of it with my arms raised in exaltation. Good photo opportunity. I'm able to clamber on top of the rock, just barely. Crouching there I decide that standing up is not a good idea. I'm afraid my legs will collapse, I'll fall off and land on my head. So I just hold the crouch with arms raised and my biggest smile on my face. I'm totally

159

overwhelmed by a natural endorphin high. Euphoric. The last time I felt like this was when my children were born.

Helen and John Stergius with Bob at the finish line. Photo by Judy Esser.

Judy and Walt Esser with Bob at the finish line. Photo by Helen Stergius

I manage to hop off the rock without injuring myself, then my friends encircle me. Shaking hands. Grinning Hugging. Everyone talking at once. Ulli and Traudl are here. He is limping badly. I ask him if he broke something, and he replies characteristically, "Oh, it's nothing. I'll be all right in a few days."

Charlie Thorn congratulates me. "Way to go, Bob. I got your time at 50:36:04."

"Thanks, Charlie. How did you do? Top ten?"

"No, not quite. I managed to finish in sixteenth place, just over 35 hours."

"Hey, that's fantastic."

Blake Wood, a big grin on his face, offers his hand. "Congratulations, Bob. You were out there a long time." This shows the kind of guy Blake is. He won the race, but he makes the effort to be at the finish line to greet the last runner.

"Thanks man, here we are, first and last together. Congratulations yourself on winning the race. What was your time?"

"30:10:58."

"Wow, amazing. Twenty hours faster than me."

Even if I had run in Blake's shoes and won the race I couldn't be any happier.

The excitement finally dies down. Walt is right next to me. I'm still wearing my gore-tex suit.

"Why don't you take off some of your clothes. Do you want to get cleaned up before the awards ceremony?"

"Ya, I can shower in the locker room next to the gym. I cut my hand too. I'll have to get it fixed up."

When I unpin my number from my vest I notice for the first time that someone has written "This is your year Bob" on the back. I'll bet it was Carolyn Erdman. She was right. It makes me feel even happier that Carolyn was thinking of me and wishing me well before the race. That's typical of her spirit.

161

There's no soap in the shower and having both hands injured makes scrubbing my body tricky, but at least the hot water washes off the top layer of grime. Usually, it takes two or three showers to make me feel reasonably clean after running 100 miles.

Quickly, I pull on a pair of shorts and a t-shirt so I can join the crowd of runners, crew members, and well wishers in the gym. The first person I encounter is Roger Wiegand. Roger is absolutely ebullient, more animated than I have ever seen him. He was the last of 59 official finishers in 47:51:25 and he can't stop talking. I was the last of five unofficial finishers and I can't decide what to do next-soak up the *joie de vivre*, eat, or find medical attention for my hand. Spying Andi Kron, I decide on the latter.

Showing her the damage, I ask, "Hey, Andi. I cut my hand on a tree. Is there anyone here who can sew it up?" At this point Dale Garland appears at Andi's shoulder. He has a scowl on his face. Not like the usual smiling Dale. I assume it's fatigue from his race directing duties. Andi looks concerned.

"Dr. Winkler has left, but there's an EMS person around here someplace," she says. "I'll go find her."

Andi cuts across the crowded room and soon returns with a medic.

"What's wrong?" she asks.

I show her my hand.

"I guess we should put a bandage on that," she observes. Turning to Andi, she asks, "Do you have a medical kit?" This person is employed by Emergency Medical Services of Silverton. Why doesn't she have her bag with her? Just then Mickie Halaburt shows up. I've met her in the past. She's a physician's assistant.

Looking at my hand, she says, "We'll have to clean it thoroughly before we sew it up. Come over to my clinic in ten minutes."

That's what I like. Someone who knows her job and takes charge. Before I go over to the clinic, I need to get something to eat. My finish line adrenaline is wearing off, and I'll need some energy to stay on my feet for a while longer. Standing in the buffet line, I feel a tap on my shoulder. Turning around I find Dale Garland looking like the Dark Side of The Force.

"I have you dropping out at Cunningham Gulch," he says.

"What?" I have heard him clearly, but my mind is trying to sort out what he means.

"I have you dropping out at Cunningham Gulch," he repeats. "You didn't make the cutoff." There must be some mistake. Maybe he missed my arrival at the Hardrock and all the excitement.

"But I finished. I just got here fifteen minutes ago."

"You left Cunningham Gulch aid station at 1:40, ten minutes after it officially closed." I guess their communication was bad. He probably hasn't been told about the aid station captain giving me permission to leave late.

"But, your man on the spot, Aaron Goldman, told me I could take my time."

"I know about that. I'm overruling him." This is dumbfounding. It's like I'm back at the pond a few miles from the finish and I can't tell the difference between reality and fiction. But this isn't the beauty of nature I'm contemplating. It's the ugliness of petty bureaucracy.

"This isn't fair. I finished the race fair and square and I didn't break any rules." My voice is rising and I'm confused, but under the chaos of feelings this information has aroused in me, I'm still happy. The bedrock fact is that I finished the race and no one can take that away from me.

Dale decides that he doesn't want to continue arguing with me in front of a crowd of people so he says, "See me after the awards ceremony. We'll talk about it."

Walt is alongside me. He says, "They told us about this before you finished, but we told them they would have to give you the news. None of us was going to tell you that you DNFed."

"That's cause I didn't. I don't care what he says; I finished the race."

Just then I notice Charlie Thorn talking to some other runners. He greeted me at the finish line. He told me what my time was. I've had many conversations with Charlie about the race. He's on the race committee. He's a guy I can trust.

Walking over to the group, I ask, "Hey, Charlie. Dale is saying I DNFed at Cunningham, but Aaron gave me permission to continue. Can you speak to the race committee on my behalf?"

Charlie responds, "Don't worry; I keep the official race records." That sounds good, but it's a little vague.

"You saw me at the finish line. I agree it was unofficial and I'll take my asterisk, but I didn't DNF."

Again he assures me, "I'm the record keeper. Don't worry about it."

I guess that's all I'll get out of Charlie at this point. I have more pressing needs, so I return to the food line. With a plate full of American fried potatoes and scrambled eggs, I join my friends already sitting in a circle of chairs. Eric Erdman, Carolyn's husband, comes over to speak to me.

"Bob, I saw you at nearly every aid station and your demeanor never changed the entire race. You did a great job to finish."

"Thanks, Eric. I appreciate it. Maybe I looked the same on the outside, but I was going through some changes on the inside. How's Carolyn?"

"She's fine now that she's had some sleep. She just pooped out climbing Buffalo Boy Ridge and missed the cutoff at Cunningham."

"There's always next year."

Finishing my food, I ask Walt to drive me over to the Silverton Clinic, where Mickie sews up my hand. When that's over, I don't feel like going back to the awards ceremony at the gym, so we drive back to the Triangle Motel. It's a gray day, the sky overcast with clouds. As we arrive it starts to rain, and I finally run out of gas. Rest is what I need now. I'm in bed for the first time in 54 hours and sleep comes quickly.

In a vivid dream I'm back at Hillside Cemetery gazing across the Animas River at Kendall Mountain. A magnificent bull elk with a full set of antlers appears in a clearing on the mountainside. His tail switches signalling that he is in rut. His flanks are heavily muscled. I can see his heart beating. Moisture glistens on his nose. His eyes shine. He shakes his rack of antlers and then a shudder goes through his body. The light in his eyes dims and he drops to his knees. He melts down until all that remains is his skull with the antlers still attached. The dream ends. The ultimate reality is death.

Blake Wood after winning the 1999 Hardrock 100. Photo by Judy Esser

Betsy Kalmeyer and her pacer, Dick Curtis, at the finish line. Photo by Julie Arter

Afterword.

Fifty-nine finishers out of 110 starters constituted the second best finishing percentage in the history of the race. Ulli Kamm, Kirk Apt, and Gordon Hardman recorded their sixth completions. Blake Wood, John DeWalt, Jim Fisher, Odin Christensen, and Charlie Thorn finished their fifth Hardrocks. Blake ran the race of a lifetime. His 30:10:58 was a record for the clockwise direction and the second fastest time ever recorded for the Hardrock Hundred. In a surprising development, Hans Put caught Randy Isler in the final section of the course and finished second in 30:56:23. Randy came in third in 31:05:04.

In the finest women's Hardrock ever contested, all three of the top ladies broke Laura Vaughan's course record, and two finished in the top ten. Running scared, Betsy Kalmeyer had the fastest time of all the runners, male and female, from Cunningham Gulch to the finish. She came in sixth overall to lock up her victory in 31:55:19, a remarkable 8 hours and 48 minutes faster than her 1996 time. Sue Johnston was ninth overall in 32:37:02, and Betsy Nye finished eighteenth in 35:19:20. At 23, Emily Loman was the youngest ever Hardrock finisher in 45:27:50. Carolyn Erdman won the Mother Lode award presented annually to an individual who contributes greatly to the success of the run. Nico Solomos, the runner who was evacuated from Pole Creek aid station, recovered quickly with no ill effects.

Not all of the finishers went to great lengths to acclimatize themselves. Hans Put and Dan Curley arrived two days before the start of the event, and each of them made it all the way around. According to Tim Noakes in *Lore of Running*, it's not so much a person's VO2 max that is a good predictor of high altitude mountain running capability. Rather, performance ability at altitude is due to a person's capacity for maintaining a high rate of ventilation in response to low oxygen content in the air. In other words, people who finish Hardrock after only two days at altitude can move more air into and out of their lungs than ordinary people can. Staying well hydrated matters too.

Of course, I was upset about not being recognized as a finisher. Upon returning home I e-mailed Charlie asking him what I should do about changing my status. Helen, bless her heart, also sent e-mails on my behalf to Charlie and other Hardrock race officials. Charlie recommended writing a letter to the members of the run committee, stating my case. On Sunday, July 18, in the midst of composing my letter, I received the following e-mail message from the Hardrock 100 director:

"Hi Bob, Where to start? Hmmmmmmm. How about I'm sorry. I felt really bad last weekend about the way I handled myself at the awards ceremony. Afterall, you had just finished something that meant a lot to you and I was pretty insensitive to that accomplishment!!! So first of all, congrats on a great achievement!!!

"So now the other news; we looked at all the mitigating circumstances surrounding your finish and I'm happy to tell you that you are going to be counted as a finisher for this years run! Of course, there is this little detail about an asterisk but I'll leave getting rid of that up to you!!!

"I hope that this makes up for my actions in some way. I really do think you're 'wild and tough'!!

"Hope your feeling ok!!

"Dale Garland."

Will I attempt the Hardrock 100 again? Don't ask now. It's too soon after the race, but you never know. There's something about the San Juans; maybe it's the sound of cascading water or the way the cool morning light swaths the peaks that touches your soul and changes your life. And there's no cure for Hardrock Fever.

Desperate Dreams

Whoever said it was going to be easy wasn't in love with you.
But I'd do the same old thing all over again if I had it to do.
So hold me close just for old times sake; I don't want it to end.
What's one more kiss before we say goodbye;
What's one more night between friends.

Desperate people doing desperate things.
Lying and learning to scheme.
Desperate people thinking desperate things;
Dreaming desperate dreams.

Nobody ever loved you more than I do;
I'll never love you no less.
This ain't no way to treat a good guy like me;
I'll always give you my best.

Desperate people doing desperate things.
Lying and learning to scheme.
Desperate people thinking desperate things,
Dreaming desperate dreams.

Paul D. Costa

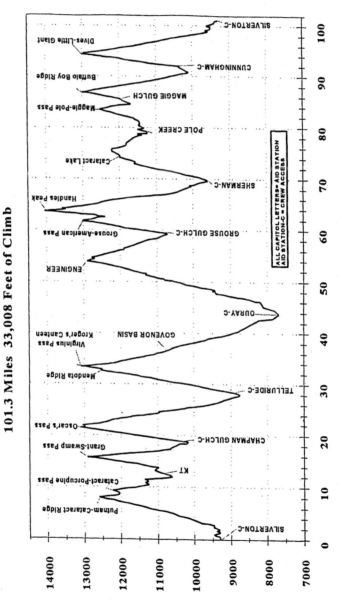

Hardrock 100 Mile Mountain Run
101.3 Miles 33,008 Feet of Climb

Hardrock Hundred 1999 Results

110 starters, 59 finishers under 48 hours, 5 unoffical finishers over 48 hours.

1	Blake Wood, M, 40, NM	30:10:56
	Clockwise Course Record	
2	Hans Put, M, 38, NY	30:56:23
3	Randy Isler, M, 42, NM	31:05:04
4	Curtis Anderson, M, 36, UT	31:22:50
5	Jim Nelson, M, 38, UT	31:54:36
6	Betsy Kalmeyer, F, 38, CO	31:55:36
	Female Course Record	
7	Scott Gordon, M, 38, NM	32:00:33
8	Tim Seminoff, M, 40, UT	32:32:59
9	Sue Johnston, F, 33, VT	32:37:02
10	Jan Fiala, M, 45, NM	33:08:05
11	Regis Shivers Jr., M, 29, OH	33:25:32
12	Kirk Apt, M, 37, CO	33:39:53
13	Andy Lapkass, M, 41, CO	33:49:44
14	Gordon Hardman, M, 48, CO	34:15:29
15	Tyler Curiel, M, 43, TX	34:27:19
16	Charlie Thorn, M, 53, NM	35:01:57
17	Alfred Bogenhuber, M, 59, CA	35:05:26
18	Betsy Nye, F, 34, CA	35:19:20
19	Steffen Buttner, M, 38, NZ	35:52:50
20	Tim Hewitt, M, 44, PA	36:17:18
21	Mark Melvin, M, 39, CA	36:22:42
22	Mike Sandlin, M, 44, TX	36:46:06
23	Eric Robinson, M, 31, CA	36:59:03
24	Mike Mitchell, M, 40, UT	37:21:16
24	Mike Tilden, M, 32, UT	37:21:16
26	Rob Youngren, M, 25, AL	37:50:48
27	Richard Ruid, M, 38, MO	38:05:00
28	Tim Neckar, M, 37, TX	38:37:53
29	Dave Dixson, M, 28, NM	38:44:55

30	Tom Rowe, M, 50, MT	38:58:06
31	Eric Pence, M, 33, CO	39:25:58
32	Lance Goss, M, 53, CA	39:30:50
33	Steve Pattillo, M, 48, NM	39:32:30
34	Mike Ehrlich, M, 36, CO	39:34:40
35	Roch Horton, M, 41, CO	39:37:02
36	Dennis Herr, M, 52, VA	39:45:15
37	Dan Curley, M, 53, CA	39:45:45
38	Jim Benike, M, 49, MN	40:15:12
39	Randy Wojno, M, 40, CO	41:23:50
40	Jim Fisher, M, 48, NM	41:51:41
41	John DeWalt, M, 63, PA	42:03:53
42	Diane Ridgway, F, 50, CO	42:37:23
43	Matt Mahoney, M, 43, FL	42:39:14
44	Bert Meyer, M, 54, CT	42:42:55
45	Odin Christensen, M, 54, CO	43:10:30
46	John McGrew, M, 41, CO	43:16:30
47	Mike Dobies, M, 38, MI	44:50:08
48	Nigel Finney, M, 52, MN	44:51:20
49	Jan Gnass, M, 49, CA	45:12:25
50	Kerry Collings, M, 50, UT	45:27:50
50	Emily Loman, F, 23, CO	45:27:50
52	Mike Thomas, M, 37, CO	45:47:38
53	Rollin Perry, M, 60, IA	45:56:12
54	Ginny LaForme, F, 49, NM	46:17:25
55	Scott Smith, M, 37, UT	46:19:31
56	Gary Wright, M, 48, WA	47:31:10
57	Jim Ballard, M, 49, MT	47:31:30
57	Ulli Kamm, M, 51, CO	47:31:30
59	Roger Wiegand, M, 56, NE	47:51:25
*	Todd Burgess, M, 30, CO	48:03:35
*	Jim Magill, M, 52, CA	48:12:58
*	Bozena Maslanka, F, 32, CA	48:33:45
*	Harry Smith, M, 50, PA	48:33:45
*	Bob Boeder, M, 57, NC	50:36:04

* Unofficial Finisher: made the cutoff at the last aid station, but finished over the 48 hour limit.

Hardrock Hundred Historical Results, 1992 - 1999

Pl	Name	Age	ST	Time	Sex	Year-Place	# Fin
1	David Horton	43	VA	29:35:48	M	93-1	4
2	Blake Wood	40	NM	30:10:58	M	99-1	5
3	Ricky Denesik	38	CO	30:12:31	M	98-1	
4	David Horton	48	VA	30:27:00	M	98-2	4
5	Mark C. McDermott	38	UK	30:33:31	M	97-1T	
6	Mark Hartell	32	UK	30:33:31	M	97-1T	2
7	Rick Trujillo	48	CO	30:44:17	M	96-1	2
8	Mark Hartell	31	UK	30:54:13	M	96-2	2
9	Hans Put	38	NY	30:56:23	M	99-2	
10	Kirk Apt	36	CO	31:03:20	M	98-3	6
11	Randy Isler	42	NM	31:05:04	M	99-3	4
12	Randy Isler	41	NM	31:14:50	M	98-4	4
13	Scott Mills	47	VA	31:16:53	M	98-5	2
14	Curtis Anderson	36	UT	31:22:50	M	99-4	
15	David Horton	46	VA	31:40:59	M	96-3	4
16	Joe Clapper	39	VA	31:47:37	M	98-6	2
17	Mark Lange	33	CO	31:53:54	M	96-4	3
18	Jim Nelson	38	UT	31:54:36	M	99-5	
19	Betsy Kalmeyer	38	CO	31:55:36	F	99-6	2
20	Scott Hirst	33	CO	32:00:13	M	94-1	
21	Scott Gordon	38	NM	32:00:33	M	99-7	
22	Randy Isler	40	NM	32:17:05	M	97-3	4
23	Rick Trujillo	46	CO	32:20:24	M	94-2	2
24	David Horton	42	VA	32:24	M	92-1	4
25	Kirk Apt	32	CO	32:29:40	M	94-3	6
26	Tim Seminoff	40	UT	32:32:59	M	99-8	
27	Charlie Thorn	47	NM	32:36:14	M	93-2	5
28	Randy Isler	39	NM	32:36:38	M	96-5	4
29	Sue Johnston	33	VT	32:37:02	F	99-9	
30	Giselher Schneider	34	GER	32:43:54	M	98-7	
31	Kirk Apt	35	CO	32:43:58	M	97-4	6
32	Mark Lange	30	CO	32:58:30	M	93-3	3
33	Jonathan Worswick	35	CA	33:01:15	M	98-8	
34	Jan Fiala	45	NM	33:08:05	M	99-10	2
35	Regis Shivers Jr.	29	OH	33:25:32	M	99-11	
36	Dennis Herr	45	VA	33:37	M	92-2	3

173

37	Kirk Apt	37	CO	33:39:53	M	99-12	6
38	Mark Heaphy	34	MT	33:41:47	M	97-5	2
39	Blake Wood	38	NM	33:43:25	M	97-6	5
40	Andy Lapkass	41	CO	33:49:44	M	99-13	
41	Mark Heaphy	31	MT	33:57:32	M	94-4	2
42	Gordon Hardman	45	CO	33:59:55	M	96-6	6
43	Gordon Hardman	48	CO	34:15:29	M	99-14	6
44	Kirk Apt	31	CO	34:21:01	M	93-4	6
45	Tyler Curiel	43	TX	34:27:19	M	99-15	
46	Paul Fuller	42	CO	34:36:15	M	94-5	
47	Scott Mills	45	VA	34:51:15	M	96-7T	2
48	Joe Clapper	37	VA	34:51:15	M	96-7T	2
49	Scott McKenzie	43	CA	34:51:19	M	98-9	
50	Thomas Nielsen	37	CA	34:52:07	M	97-7	
51	Charlie Thorn	53	NM	35:01:57	M	99-16	5
52	Alfred Bogenhuber	59	CA	35:05:26	M	99-17	
53	Gordon Hardman	46	CO	35:16:01	M	97-8	6
54	Betsy Nye	34	CA	35:19:20	F	99-18	
55	Kurt Madden	38	CA	35:29:00	M	94-6	
56	Charlie Thorn	52	NM	35:35:17	M	98-10	5
57	Kirk Apt	34	CO	35:35:50	M	96-9	6
58	Chip Lee	38	CO	35:44:16	M	93-5	3
59	Gordon Hardman	41	CO	35:47	M	92-3	6
60	Rolly Portelance	54	ONT	35:51:27	M	97-9	2
61	Gordon Hardman	43	CO	35:52:19	M	94-7	6
62	Dennis Herr	46	VA	35:52:31	M	93-6	3
63	Steffen Buttner	38	NZ	35:52:50	M	99-19	
64	Tim Hewitt	44	PA	36:17:18	M	99-20	
65	Mark Melvin	39	CA	36:22:42	M	99-21	
66	Charlie Thorn	51	NM	36:43:32	M	97-10	5
67	Mike Sandlin	44	TX	36:46:06	M	99-22	
68	Chip Lee	39	CO	36:54:10	M	94-8	3
69	Eric Robinson	31	CA	36:59:03	M	99-23	2
70	Odin Christensen	45	CO	37:08:05	M	93-7	5
71	Phil Kahn	43	CO	37:14:32	M	96-10	3
72	John Cappis	50	NM	37:19	M	92-4T	
73	Charlie Thorn	46	NM	37:19	M	92-4T	5
75	Mike Mitchell	40	UT	37:21:16	M	99-24T	
74	Mike Tilden	32	UT	37:21:16	M	99-24T	

76	Laura Vaughan	31	CA	37:22:32	F	97-11	
77	John Amies	55	UK	37:47:28	M	97-12T	
78	Craig Wilson	48	ME	37:47:28	M	97-12T	
79	Rob Youngren	25	AL	37:50:48	M	99-26	
80	Bert Meyer	48	CT	37:52:40	M	93-8	4
81	Randy Rhodes	44	CO	38:04:42	M	94-9T	5
82	Tim Beaman	43	VT	38:04:42	M	94-9T	
83	Richard Ruid	38	MO	38:05:00	M	99-27	
84	Todd Holmes	40	CO	38:10:24	M	96-11	
85	Geoff Miller	35	CO	38:16:09	M	93-9	4
86	Randy Rhodes	43	CO	38:18:06	M	93-10	5
87	Jan Fiala	44	NM	38:19:31	M	98-11	2
88	Blake Wood	35	NM	38:20:22	M	94-11	5
89	Greg Martell	41	WY	38:25:38	M	98-12	
90	Eric Robinson	30	CA	38:32:43	M	98-13	2
91	Gordon Hardman	47	CO	38:34:56	M	98-14	6
92	Tim Neckar	37	TX	38:37:53	M	99-28	
93	Margaret Smith	38	MT	38:43:09	F	94-12	2
94	Dave Dixson	28	NM	38:44:55	M	99-29	
95	Odin Christensen	44	CO	38:45	M	92-6	5
96	Randy Rhodes	47	CO	38:50:48	M	97-14	5
97	Tom Rowe	50	MT	38:58:06	M	99-30	
98	Chip Lee	43	CO	38:58:29	M	98-15	3
99	Blake Wood	39	NM	39:07:59	M	98-16	5
100	Joanne Urioste	42	NV	39:18:26	F	94-13	
101	Scott Grierson	27	ME	39:21:12	M	94-14	
102	Chris Nute	30	CO	39:21:33	M	98-17	
103	Adrian Crane	38	CA	39:22:10	M	93-11	
104	Eric Pence	33	CO	39:25:58	M	99-31	
105	Randy Rhodes	46	CO	39:26:37	M	96-12	5
106	Mark Williams	31	CA	39:29:50	M	97-15	
107	Lance Goss	53	CA	39:30:50	M	99-32	
108	Bill Laster	49	AR	39:31:14	M	98-18	
109	Steve Pattillo	48	NM	39:32:30	M	99-33	2
110	Mike Ehrlich	36	CO	39:34:40	M	99-34	
111	Roch Horton	41	CO	39:37:02	M	99-35	
112	Dennis Herr	52	VA	39:45:15	M	99-36	3
113	Dan Curley	53	CA	39:45:45	M	99-37	
114	Mark Lange	29	CO	39:55	M	92-7	3

115	Andrew Addis	42	UK	40:12:31	M	97-16T	
116	Paul McClintock	31	UK	40:12:31	M	97-16T	
117	Jim Benike	49	MN	40:15:12	M	99-38	
118	John McGrew	39	CO	40:26:03	M	97-18	3
119	John Demorest	46	CA	40:26:58	M	97-19	
120	Larry Alire	50	CO	40:33:45	M	97-20	2
121	Odin Christenson	48	CO	40:35:50	M	96-13	5
122	Douglas McKeever	45	WA	40:38:15	M	93-12	
123	Betsy Kalmeyer	35	CO	40:43:13	F	96-14	2
124	Geoff Miller	38	CO	40:55:06	M	96-15	4
125	Eliza McLean	32	NC	40:57:57	F	98-19T	
126	Steve Simmons	32	WV	40:57:57	M	98-19T	
127	Mark McDermott	31	CO	41:04:55	M	93-13	
128	Blake Wood	37	NM	41:11:36	M	96-16	5
129	Steve Pattillo	47	NM	41:18:55	M	98-21	2
130	Martyn Greaves	33	UK	41:22:34	M	93-14	2
131	Randy Wojno	40	CO	41:23:50	M	99-39	2
132	Nick Williams	50	AR	41:26:46	M	93-15	2
133	Mike Dobies	36	MI	41:31:46	M	97-21	2
134	Margaret Smith	37	MT	41:38:38	F	93-16	2
135	Bert Meyer	49	CT	41:50:26	M	94-15	4
136	Jim Fisher	48	NM	41:51:41	M	99-40	5
137	James Benike	47	MN	42:01:39	M	97-22T	
138	Matthew Janney	42	OR	42:01:39	M	97-22T	
139	John DeWalt	63	PA	42:03:53	M	99-41	5
140	Steve McCormick	49	CO	42:06:55	M	94-17T	
141	Garry Curry	40	CO	42:06:55	M	94-17T	2
142	Lew Larson	40	CO	42:06:55	M	94-17T	
143	Jim Fisher	45	NM	42:12:30	M	96-17	5
144	Randy Rhodes	42	CO	42:26	M	92-8T	5
145	Thomas Knutson	41	MN	42:26	M	92-8T	
146	Diane Ridgway	50	CO	42:37:23	F	99-42	2
147	Matt Mahoney	43	FL	42:39:14	M	99-43	
148	Jon MacManus	45	CO	42:40:26	M	96-18	
149	Bert Meyer	54	CT	42:42:55	M	99-44	4
150	Jim Fisher	43	NM	42:59:59	M	94-19	5
151	Garry Curry	42	CO	43:08:06	M	96-19T	2
152	Randy Wojno	36	CO	43:08:06	M	96-19T	2
153	Odin Christensen	54	CO	43:10:30	M	99-45	5

154	Thomas Green	45	MD	43:12:43	M	96-21	
155	Julie Westland-Litus	35	CO	43:14:50	F	93-17	4
156	John McGrew	41	CO	43:16:30	M	99-46	3
157	Odin Christensen	49	CO	43:20:05	M	97-25T	5
158	Geoff Miller	39	CO	43:20:05	M	97-25T	4
159	Milan Milanovich	37	CH	43:20:05	M	97-25T	
160	Jim Fisher	42	NM	43:21:10	M	93-18	5
161	Jim Fisher	47	NM	43:26:26	M	98-22	5
162	Julie Westland-Litus	36	CO	43:41:47	F	94-21T	4
163	Steve Tilley	47	AR	43:41:47	M	94-21T	2
164	Phil Kahn	41	CO	43:41:47	M	94-21T	3
165	Hal Winton	64	CA	43:48:16	M	96-22	
166	Burgess Harmer	51	NV	43:48:33	M	93-19	
167	David Lygre	53	WA	43:49:12	M	96-23	
168	Matt Hornung	40	CO	43:51:51	M	97-27	2
169	Hans van Willigen	60	MA	43:51:53	M	98-23	
170	John Addis	41	UK	44:08:10	M	96-24	
171	Mark Spangler	45	MN	44:08:48	M	97-28	
172	Mary Lou Morgan-Pentasuglio	43	CO	44:13:42	F	97-29	2
173	Kristina Irvin	40	CA	44:32:07	F	98-24	
174	Bobby Keogh	49	NM	44:32:24	M	98-25	
175	Dick West	51	MI	44:37:12	M	93-20T	
176	Eugene Trahern	30	WA	44:37:12	M	93-20T	
177	Ulrich Kamm	45	GER	44:38:15	M	93-22	6
178	John McGrew	38	CO	44:41:00	M	96-25	3
179	Cliff Davies	59	ONT	44:46:16	M	94-24T	
180	Rolly Partelance	51	ONT	44:46:16	M	94-24T	2
181	John Nale	48	CO	44:46:16	M	94-24T	
182	Dick Curtis	52	CO	44:48:45	M	97-30	2
183	Don Thompson	55	CO	44:48:49	M	93-23	3
184	Mike Dobies	38	MI	44:50:00	M	99-47	2
185	Nigel Finney	52	MN	44:51:20	M	99-48	
186	Larry Alire	51	CO	44:53:58	M	98-26T	2
187	Phil Kahn	45	CO	44:53:58	M	98-26T	3
188	Diane Ridgway	47	CO	44:58:45	F	96-26	2
189	John DeWalt	61	PA	45:06:54	M	97-31	5
190	Kerry Collings	49	UT	45:11:46	M	98-28	2
191	Jan Gnass	49	CA	45:12:25	M	99-49	
192	Geoff Miller	36	CO	45:21:22	M	94-26	4

193	Allan Czecholinski	49	WI	45:22:25	M	96-27	
194	Brick Robbins	38	CA	45:25:07	M	98-29	
195	Emily Loman	23	CO	45:27:50	F	99-50T	
196	Kerry Collings	50	UT	45:27:50	M	99-50T	2
197	Alfred Kroeger	32	CO	45:35	M	92-10	3
198	Mary Lou Morgan-Pentasuglio	42	CO	45:37:13	F	96-28	2
199	Ian Hutcheson	40	CAN	45:42:07	M	96-29T	
200	Matt Hornung	39	CO	45:42:07	M	96-29T	2
201	Jason Hodde	28	IN	45:45:07	M	98-30	
202	Nancy Hamilton	43	MD	45:47	F	92-11T	
203	Rick Hamilton	42	MD	45:47	M	92-11T	
204	Mike Thomas	37	CO	45:47:38	M	99-52	
205	Kevin O'Grady	34	OH	45:53:43	M	93-24	3
206	Rollin Perry	60	IA	45:56:12	M	99-53	4
207	Ulrich Kamm	44	GER	46:03	M	92-13	6
208	Kevin O'Grady	33	OH	46:03	M	92-14	3
209	Julie Westland-Litus	38	CO	46:08:15	F	96-32T	4
210	Charles Haraway	48	CO	46:08:15	M	96-32T	
211	Richard Hypio	40	CO	46:08:15	M	96-32T	
212	Clark Chesbro	35	CO	46:08:15	M	96-32T	2
213	Carl Yates	65	CO	46:15:26	M	93-25	
214	Ginny LaForme	49	NM	46:17:25	F	99-54	2
215	Jose Wilkie	31	KY	46:19:14	M	94-27	
216	Scott Smith	37	UT	46:19:31	M	99-55	
217	Rollin Perry	57	IA	46:21:40	M	96-35	4
218	Roland Martin	43	NV	46:24	M	92-15	
219	Clark Chesbro	33	CO	46:26:03	M	94-28	2
220	Bert Meyer	51	CT	46:27:22	M	96-36	4
221	Ulrich Kamm	48	GER	46:30:22	M	96-37T	6
222	Dana Roueche	39	CO	46:30:22	M	96-37T	2
223	Dana Roueche	40	CO	46:31:45	M	97-32	2
224	John DeWalt	62	PA	46:32:36	M	98-31	5
225	Suzi Thibeault	49	CA	46:45:28	F	97-33	
226	Rollin Perry	59	IA	46:45:54	M	98-32T	4
227	Jim Ballard	48	MT	46:45:54	M	98-32T	3
228	Rollin Perry	58	IA	46:45:56	M	97-34	4
229	Julie Westland-Litus	34	CO	46:47	F	92-16	4
230	Nick Williams	51	AR	46:49:10	M	94-29	2
231	Steve Tilley	50	AR	46:51:09	M	97-35	2

232	Dan Whittemore	45	NH	46:56:13	M	97-36	
233	John DeWalt	60	PA	46:58:23	M	96-39T	5
234	Kawika Spaulding	42	HI	46:58:23	M	96-39T	
235	Ulrich Kamm	49	CO	47:03:10	M	97-37T	6
236	Jim Ballard	47	MT	47:03:10	M	97-37T	3
237	Tony Grappo	43	NV	47:08:53	M	94-30	
238	Don Thompson	54	CO	47:15	M	92-17	3
239	Alfred Kroeger	33	CO	47:15:51	M	93-26	3
240	Dick Curtis	53	CO	47:19:19	M	98-34	2
241	Alfred Kroeger	34	CO	47:21:12	M	94-31	3
242	Don Thompson	56	CO	47:27:30	M	94-32	3
243	Gary Wright	48	WA	47:31:10	M	99-56	
245	Ulli Kamm	51	CO	47:31:30	M	99-57T	6
244	Jim Ballard	49	MT	47:31:30	M	99-57T	3
246	Ginny LaForme	48	NM	47:37:06	F	98-35T	2
247	Stuart Johnson	39	KS	47:37:06	M	98-35T	
248	Joel Zucker	44	NY	47:37:17	M	98-37	3
249	Arthur Schwartz	46	CO	47:39	M	92-18	
250	Lee Schmidt	54	CA	47:43:48	M	94-33	
251	Ulrich Kamm	46	GER	47:46:26	M	94-34T	6
252	Martyn Greaves	36	UK	47:46:26	M	94-34T	2
253	Bozena Maslanka	32	CA	47:49:59	F	98-38	
254	Joel Zucker	43	NY	47:50:01	M	97-39	3
255	John DeWalt	58	PA	47:50:21	M	94-36T	5
256	Kevin O'Grady	35	OH	47:50:21	M	94-36T	3
257	Joel Zucker	42	NY	47:50:41	M	96-41	3
258	Roger Wiegand	56	NE	47:51:25	M	99-59	
259	Richard Senelly	52	HI	47:59:35	M	96-42	
*	Todd Burgess	30	CO	48:03:35	M	99-60	
*	Suzi Thibeault	48	CA	48:05:05	F	96-43	
*	Jim Magill	52	CA	48:12:58	M	99-61	
*	Carl Yates	69	CA	48:21:36	M	97-40	
*	Bozena Maslanka	32	CA	48:33:45	F	99-62	
*	Harry Smith	50	PA	48:33:45	M	99-63	
*	Bob Boeder	57	NC	50:36:04	M	99-64	
*	Fred Vance	45	CA	51:08:00	M	98-39	
*	Matt Mahoney	42	FL	51:08:00	M	98-40	

179

HARDROCK ENDURANCE RUN

100 MILE

WILD & TOUGH

Order Form

To order additional copies, fill out this form and send it along with your check or money order to: Bob Boeder, 2013 Mango Cir., Fayetteville, NC 28304.

Cost per copy $12.95 plus $1.50 P&H.

Ship _____ copies of *Hardrock Fever* to:

Name_____

Address:_____

_____

_____

❏   **Check box for signed copy**